COACHING WINNING SOFTBALL

COACHING WINNING SOFTBALL

LOREN
"CHICK"
WALSH

Contemporary Books, Inc.
Chicago

Library of Congress Cataloging in Publication Data

Walsh, Loren.
  Coaching winning softball.

  Includes index.
  1. Softball coaching.   I. Title.
GV881.W32   1979   796.357′8   78-73681
ISBN 0-8092-7456-6
ISBN 0-8092-7455-8 pbk.

R0040063789

Copyright © 1979 by Loren Walsh
All rights reserved
Published by Contemporary Books, Inc.
180 North Michigan Avenue, Chicago, Illinois 60601
Manufactured in the United States of America
Library of Congress Catalog Card Number: 78-73681
International Standard Book Number: 0-8092-7456-6 (cloth)
                                                   0-8092-7455-8 (paper)

Published simultaneously in Canada by
Beaverbooks
953 Dillingham Road
Pickering, Ontario L1W 1Z7
Canada

To my daughter
CATHY MARIE

Contents

COACHING WINNING SOFTBALL

1

Coaching—Leading and Communicating

Is a good coach always a winning coach? In the minds of most spectators, professional, college, and high school coaches, a winning coach and a good coach are synonymous. Vince Lombardi believed that winning was not only important, it was the only way to think.

A well-known quote hangs in many gymnasiums and locker rooms: "It's not important who won or lost, but how you played the game." Endless quotes and statements like this are used to spur sports competitors.

One of the most detrimental quotes to the young competitor's growth was made by a famous baseball manager: "Nice guys finish last." First, it isn't true. And second, that kind of attitude tends to corrupt and mislead young people from grasping the concept of competitive sports.

Coaching objectives and responsibilities are substantially different for various levels of competition. A professional coach or manager must be capable of working efficiently with several assistant coaches. He must accurately recognize potential of new prospects. He has to be a good organizer, administrator, and motivator. His prime objective is to win games which will attract large crowds and turn franchises into profitable properties.

Most college coaches are under the same pressures. The college coach must be a good recruiter, a good public relations man, a motivator, an administrator, and a winner. Although the professional must be able to teach and instruct, he doesn't have to put as much effort in this area as the college coach.

For the most part, the high school coach also has pressure to be a winner. However, he isn't concerned with recruiting, doesn't have the burden of dealing with alumni groups, and has little concern for the financial return on his team's won and loss record. His major role is to be an instructor of fundamentals. Unfortunately, too many coaches lose sight of this role. They are often frustrated athletes trying to emulate Vince Lombardi, John Wooden, and Casey Stengel. These people spend far too much time trying to instill a winning attitude instead of instructing.

Young children are frequently turned away from organized sports due to overzealous coaches. In fact, verbal abuse can be extremely detrimental to the young player's future in organized sports. There have been far too many needless tongue lashings and nonconstructive criticisms dished out by poorly trained teachers and coaches at the grade-school level.

Just how much effort should be placed on winning is difficult to assess. Nevertheless, the desire to win is important to any competitive activity. If it weren't, there would be no reason to keep score. No way can we dismiss the fact that winning is a measure of success. However, it must not be emphasized to the point where the youngster is berated.

TEAM EFFORT

Team sports are excellent for teaching individuals how to work together. When each member performs to his maximum capability in a cooperative effort, the team attains optimum performance. When one or more fails to put forth his best effort, group success is directly affected.

Most individuals in our society must function as a member of a group whether they work for a company, the government, or an educational institution. The level of performance achieved by the group depends significantly on how well the individuals work together.

Like all sports softball has various levels of competition. This book is directed to each of those levels, both in fast and slow pitch. Although some of the material presented will deal with advanced strategy, methods for teaching fundamentals are covered for each position.

LEADING

When you are the head coach, employ a natural and deliberate style. Don't try to be something you aren't. Copying the style of someone who has been successful does not mean that it is the best for you. A natural style is the most desirable and effective. Nevertheless, it's possible you may possess a few characteristics that are neither endearing nor useful. Identify them and try to get rid of them.

All coaches run into personnel problems during the season. When they arise, don't procrastinate. Face them squarely. Overlooking little problems often results in bigger ones. Assess the situation calmly, carefully. Then work out a way of handling it. Above all, don't flail out recklessly while squashing a little problem or you may create other difficulties that would never have come up.

It's best not to place blame on one individual. Your objective is to improve team performance. When this perspective is clear, one can deal with problems on a straightforward basis.

Should you be fortunate enough to have assistants, use them. Let them be an important part of the organization. Often the assistant may detect the start of a problem long before the head coach. If assistants feel they are an integral part of the program, they are more likely to volunteer their help in a positive way. Delegate specific responsibilities to them, sometimes letting them run the show.

When the assistant understands the system and feels comfortable in the organization he will contribute substantially to the team's performance. Furthermore, if an emergency arises, the assistant can take over without jeopardizing the team's effectiveness.

FOLLOWING

An assistant coach must be a good follower, not just obedient or servile. It's not an easy thing to do, however. The good assistant strives for the same results as the head coach. The desire for the same results must exist.

A good assistant takes the time to insure that he or she thoroughly understands the intent of the head coach. However, the assistant must not become the boss to players. Instead, he should stick to his assigned area of activity. This prescription will not restrict effectiveness or curtail creativity; it merely eliminates confusion in players' minds.

Good assistants expand their knowledge, listen, and follow the leader's requests. Poor assistants spend time carving a piece of the leader's cave. Contradiction or destructive criticism seldom accomplishes anything, except delaying objectives.

Following is not learned just to satisfy a temporary obligation on the way to becoming the leader. One should never completely break from the role of follower. You may reach the level where your leader is the president, the owner, or sponsor of the organization. You may be promoted to the top of the heap. But even the president of the country must follow the peoples' wishes. Always work at following. Leading will then take care of itself.

COMMUNICATING

Communication is an exchange of information which is expressed, received, and assimilated so there is a complete understanding by the parties involved. Many experts compare communications to a broadcasting system. When no receivers pick up the station's signals, communication is incomplete. Both sending and receiving units must be operating properly before communication takes place.

The coach in softball is usually the sending station. He or she beams out ideas and instructions to the assistants and players. Most coaches believe that once the message is sent out it is automatically received. But remember, the sender gives out information effectively only when the receiver is properly tuned in. When the station spews out static or speaks in a foreign language, the receiver fails to get the message.

Good communication requires that the receiver not only hears the message but also understands it. Therefore, the sender must also be a good listener to determine if the receiver understands the transmission. An efficient communicator not only learns what and how to say it, but also clearly interprets what the other person is saying.

IMPROVING COMMUNICATION

Constant effort should be exerted to upgrade your communication skills. Although there are many ways to develop an improvement program, one of the easiest is to make an outline and follow it.

A. Plan: Carefully analyze how you will present as well as share instruction.
B. Explain: Speak clearly and accentuate important points. Repeat if necessary.
C. Verify: Review and analyze what the other person means.
D. Evaluate: Use follow-up methods to confirm that there is mutual understanding between concerned parties.

Planning Suggestions

Keep the following points in mind. If necessary, write them down.

A. Select the best time to discuss your subject.
B. Determine exactly what you want to accomplish in a specific discussion.
C. Decide how to introduce the topics.
D. Establish what major topics should be stressed.
E. Determine ahead of time if listeners' ideas should also be sought during the discussion.
F. Analyze the individual or group prior to the session.

How to Explain

A. Use words that are compatible with the level of understanding of the people involved.
B. Employ clearly defined phrases that are free of idioms which may be foreign to the participants.
C. Clearly identify subjects to be discussed.
D. Arouse the interest of the listeners, particularly at the beginning of the session.
E. Voice tones should be adjusted to specific situations.
F. Eliminate unnecessary or trivial details.

Listening

One of the best ways to improve listening skills is by practice. While talking to your immediate listener or listeners, carefully watch what you do during the listening portion of the conversation. Maybe you are thinking ahead of what you intend to say rather than concentrat-

COMMUNICATIONS SELF-CHECK LIST

	Often	*Occasionally*	*Rarely*
1. Plan ahead what I will say	☐	☐	☐
2. Find out if players understand me	☐	☐	☐
3. Avoid arguments and conflict of opinion whenever possible	☐	☐	☐
4. Always review what speaker said	☐	☐	☐
5. Make use of written material to supplement oral instruction	☐	☐	☐
6. Use group meetings as regular communication aid	☐	☐	☐
7. Talk over individual problems in private	☐	☐	☐
8. Listen carefully to questions	☐	☐	☐
9. Listen with compassion to problems and complaints	☐	☐	☐
10. Consider individual personalities during instruction or constructive criticism	☐	☐	☐

ing on the speaker's message. Another common error of the listener is to interrupt before the speaker has finished. The following tips should help you understand what the speaker is trying to say rather than what you think he is trying to say.

A. Do not assume or anticipate.
B. Work to understand the speaker's need and reason for speaking.
C. Don't react immediately with comments or expressions. Allow the speaker to get the message across.
D. Use follow-up:
  1. Check back with players or assistants to see if they really meant what you heard.
  2. Watch for effects of follow-up to see if performance improves.
  3. Look for attitude changes within the individual or group.

Communication Self-Checklist

A. Plan ahead what to say.
B. Find out if players understand.
C. Avoid conflict whenever possible.
D. Double-check and review what speaker said.
E. Make use of written means to supplement oral instructions.
F. Use group meetings regularly.
G. Talk over individual problems in private.
H. Listen carefully to questions.
I. Listen with compassion to problems and complaints.
J. Consider individual personalities during instructions or constructive criticism.

2

Coaching— Managing Time

MANAGING TIME

A coach is much like the manager of a business. He or she must schedule practice so that optimum results are obtained. One of the best ways to accomplish this is to draw up a schedule and review the results of each practice afterward.

Suggestions:
A. Formulate a plan for each practice.
B. List the things you expect to accomplish.
C. Set priorities.
  1. Must—Things which are absolutely essential.
  2. Should—Areas that require work but are less urgent than the "Must" category.
  3. Can—Activities which should be done if time permits.

DELEGATION OF RESPONSIBILITY

Head coaches who appear flustered and hurried are those who try to do everything themselves.

Suggestions:
A. Like anything else, learning to delegate takes practice. Start by selecting one of your regular duties and let an assistant handle it.
B. Review the planned practice session each time and check those items that can be handled by others.
C. Always delegate by expected results. Explain what you want done rather than what the assistant should do. Allow the assistant some leeway in how he or she obtains results.
D. Assign as many tasks as possible once the

assistant feels comfortable in handling them.

E. Give the assistant enough authority to complete the job.

F. Make it clear to all assistants and players to whom a specific task has been assigned.

G. Hold occasional reviews with assistants to see if they are progressing satisfactorily.

DEVELOPING TALENT

Successful coaches know that training and teaching should be performed systematically. Systematic development means that a coach recognizes the player's capabilities, what must be taught, and the results expected. Once the player's capabilities are analyzed and training needs established, the coach then applies training techniques tailored to each individual.

HOW TO RECOGNIZE NEEDS

Coaching and training problems are right in front of your eyes. Watch individual characteristics that need attention. Although experienced coaches are usually capable of quickly detecting deficiencies and mistakes, there is always room for learning. For example, it is sometimes effective to compare an outstanding player to one who has a problem. Basic mistakes are many times isolated faster by this technique.

EMPLOY YARDSTICKS

List player capabilities and rate each category—(1) superior, (2) good, (3) weak.

The capabilities guide is a simple but effective way to determine where maximum work should be placed. Capability guides should be reviewed periodically to check progress.

INSTRUCTING

With proper instruction a young player with average talent should show steady improvement. However, the amount and speed of improvement depends on the skill of the instructor.

Prepare the player or players so they realize you are trying to help them become better players. Too many coaches give incomplete instructions and yell at mistakes so often that the player has a tendency to disregard the message. It's a good practice on occasion to take a player aside and explain that constructive criticism is meant to improve his or her skill. It is not intended to be a bawling out.

Use a Logical and Regular Sequence

A. Tell the individual what the purpose is, e.g., where and how to throw from a catcher's position in order to catch a runner trying to steal second base.

CAPABILITIES GUIDE

Date: ____	Hitting (Power)	Hitting (average)	Bunting	Throwing (Strength)	Throwing (accuracy)	Fielding	Running	
Bob C.	1	3	2	2	3	1	3	
Frank T.	3	1	1	1	1	1	1	
Bill S.	3	3	2	1	1	1	1	
Ray H.	1	1	2	3	3	1	3	
Jim A.	2	2	3	1	3	2	2	
								Code: 1. Superior 2. Good 3. Weak

B. Show the player how it's done. This may be accomplished by a demonstration, with pictures, film, videotape, etc.
C. Explain each detail of how the action is completed.
D. Let the individual try it.
E. Critique the performance immediately and compliment the player if it's well done.
F. Repeat the routine occasionally and check for progress. Watch carefully to see that the individual does not pick up a bad habit.
 1. Evaluate performance in total.
 2. Pinpoint where he is doing well.
 3. Work on areas that need improvement.

LEARNING PRINCIPLES

Good coaches will apply the following learning principles:

Know your players. Take into consideration that no two people are alike. They have differences in family and cultural backgrounds, ability, experience, interest, and desire.

Provide motivation. For a player to improve, he must be interested. Interest is created by a skillful coach who inspires the desire for self-improvement.

Learn by doing. Teaching, showing, observing are steps to the ladder of success. However, skill development only starts when the player genuinely participates. Although practice sessions are extremely important, they can be overdone. The game is the real testing ground for measuring performance and development.

Build on strengths. Players and good teams develop more rapidly when the coach knows what each person does best and plays them in the position most suited to their specific abilities.

Create a learning climate. Learning operates efficiently only when the proper environment is present. A good teacher creates this type of climate by his or her attitude toward people. A good coach shows concern for the pupil's improvement and constantly strives to better his own performance.

PRACTICE SESSIONS

Different coaches use different plans for conducting practices. Generally a practice session is more productive if it's organized. The following week-long practice schedule is merely a guide and should not be considered the only approach to practice planning.

Personnel *Time* *Activity*

Monday

Entire Team — 15 minutes — Preliminary warm-up, play catch and informal jogging and running.
Note: A preliminary warm-up period is used as a short-time buffer until most of the players arrive. During this period, players should be cautioned not to throw hard or do fast wind sprints.

Entire Team — 15 minutes — Organized loosening-up drills (to be led by head coach or assistant).
Note: Moderate calisthenics and wind sprints are good for this type of routine.

Entire Team — 60 minutes — Batting practice.
Note: All players should be kept moving during batting practice. For routine batting practice, the pitcher should throw at about ¾ speed. If possible, a catcher should be used, because this gives the pitcher a better target, saves time, and is safer. In order to keep things moving quickly, allow each batter six to ten fair balls. Keep a back-up man (usually the next hitter) near the pitching rubber to collect balls from the outfielders and infielders. This man should hand the balls to the pitcher, saving time and reducing pitcher fatigue.
 While the hitter is up, an assistant coach can be hitting grounders to the infielders. At the same time an assistant or another player should be hitting fly balls and grounders to the outfielders.

Entire Team — 30 minutes — Fielding practice.
With catcher, pitcher, infielders, and outfielders in position, start fielding practice by hitting balls to the outfielders. Many coaches fail to include the pitchers during this drill. This is a good time to teach the pitcher how to back up the proper base. Hit approximately ten balls to each outfielder. Mix these hits with grounders and fly balls. Each fielder should throw to second, third, and home. After the outfield drill is completed work on infield drills.

Personnel	Time	Activity
		Each fielder should have the opportunity to handle ten to fifteen balls. How the drill routine is handled should be up to each coach.

Tuesday

Personnel	Time	Activity
Infielders Catchers Pitchers	15 minutes 60 minutes	Organized loosening-up drills. Special batting practice. In a special batting practice session, begin by having the pitcher throw at ¾ speed on the first round. Also, allow each batter six to ten fairly hit balls. On the second round, allow each batter eight to twelve swings and have the pitcher throw at full speed using an assortment of stuff. Have enough pitchers available to keep from overfatiguing the pitchers.
Infielders Catchers Pitchers	10 minutes	Short infield drill. Finish infield workout with a quick infield routine. Let infielders go home.
Outfielders Catchers Pitchers	35 minutes	Routine batting practice. Have pitcher throw ¾ speed and allow each ten to fifteen fairly hit balls.

Wednesday

Personnel	Time	Activity
Outfielders Catchers Pitchers	15 minutes 60 minutes 15 minutes	Organized loosening-up drills. Special batting practice (use same system for special batting practice as described for infielders previously). Short outfield drill (use this time for general outfield drill).
Infielders Catchers Pitchers	30 minutes	Routine batting practice.

Thursday

Personnel	Time	Activity
Entire Team	15 minutes	Preliminary warm-up.
Entire Team	15 minutes	Organized loosening-up drills.
Entire Team	45 minutes	General batting practice.
Entire Team	45 minutes	Fielding practice. Use regular routine previously described, plus cover some of the special areas that need attention. This may include throwing to the proper relay man by the outfielders and backing up infielders and other outfielders. Infield may work on taking outfield relay throws and covering bunts, etc.
Entire Team	15 minutes	Review of practices. This time is used to discuss problems and to prepare for future games. Special practices may be scheduled at this time.

Although planning is important to the success of any team, each coach or manager develops his or her own individual teaching methods. A technique that is good for one may be completely wrong for another.

Practice sessions are learning experiences and should be made interesting as well as fun, particularly for the young participant. Many coaches forget this aspect. Far too many practice sessions turn into four hours of boring drills.

All coaches are faced with a variety of talent and therefore must create ideas that prevent practice from becoming monotonous. Those players requiring more work on fundamentals can be asked to practice a little earlier than those more advanced. Dividing batting practice into two or three sessions can even things up. Requesting outfielders, pitchers, infielders, and catchers to report at different times keeps things moving. There are many things a creative coach can do to improve learning in the game of softball.

3

Pitching Basics

Experts in fast pitch contend that pitching is 75 to 90 percent of the game. In other words, without a top-notch pitcher a fast-pitch team has little chance of winning the majority of their games.

Regardless of the sport, proper instruction must begin when the contestant is young. In recent years, the Olympic games have demonstrated that gold medal winners for the most part received intensive instruction at an early age.

Without question, the recent decline in the number of fast-pitch teams in the U.S. is due to an absence of good pitchers. This is because young pitchers are not being developed as rapidly as they had been during the 1930-1950 era.

Certainly natural ability is a requirement in developing the outstanding pitcher. A youngster with a strong arm and natural coordination has a definite advantage. Nevertheless, a youngster with average talent and desire can be taught the fundamentals that will prepare him for becoming a fine fast-pitch hurler.

PHYSICAL TRAITS

What physical traits are desirable for the fast-pitch pitcher? This question comes up frequently in coaching. For one thing, size is a definite plus. Although there are exceptions, most great pitchers have been big men or women. Long arms and good upper-body coordination are very important. Large hands with long fingers are an advantage due to the size of the twelve-inch softball. Endurance also plays a big role in the pitcher's physical makeup. A strong set of legs tops off the desirable points.

While quickness is important in baseball, it's not that critical in fast pitch. The fast-pitch pitcher is not required to cover first base on

Large hands and long fingers are a distinct advantage.

balls hit to the first baseman. It fact, one of the outstanding pitchers in this game was crippled.

MENTAL PREPARATION

Proper mental attitude can be just as significant as physique. Controlled temperament characterizes most outstanding pitchers. Coaches must emphasize attitude when developing the young pitcher.

More than any other position, stress accompanies the physical strain of pitching. Remaining calm through difficulties helps a pitcher become a winner. Many coaches fail to consider this when working with the rookie pitcher. During early development, a coach who is alert at recognizing attitude deficiencies can significantly help to work out these problems.

Eliminating temper tantrums and depression are just as crucial as correcting poor physical habits.

During a game, a questionable umpire's call, taunts, and kidding by opponents or spectators may have an effect on a pitcher's performance. Some pitchers are bothered by errors committed by their teammates. Incidents of this nature are

typical. Consequently, the pitcher must accept this.

When the pitcher gains a reputation for being temperamental, opposing teams will take advantage of this deficiency. As soon as a pitcher shows any emotion of this type, players and spectators will react. As a result, taunts and comments not only upset the pitcher, but ordinarily cause a negative reaction upon other team members.

DEDICATION

Desire and dedication are not easily taught. However, these characteristics, or lack of them, are easily recognizable. They are qualities a coach should note. A youngster who aspires to pitching but lacks desire is like a monotone trying to become a vocalist.

Determination is indispensable in developing a good pitcher. Years of practice must be gained by the individual wishing to pitch for top-flight fast-pitch clubs. Success is frequently preceded by failure and frustration. For some it may mean experiencing losing seasons and playing with scrub teams in obscure leagues.

When a coach has an individual with natural pitching talent but who lacks desire, his job is not an easy one. Whenever possible, the coach should use examples and case histories that demonstrate success achieved through hard work. There is no question that an unmotivated individual must be pushed and encouraged. In some instances it may require extra practice sessions, concentrated work on fundamentals. Often an unmotivated individual requires recognition in order to motivate himself since he may be easily discouraged.

BUILD SELF-CONFIDENCE

Self-confidence is another trait not easily taught but essential to pitchers. A young pitcher lacking this trait must be frequently encouraged and praised. However, he must never be babied.

A pitcher with self-confidence can withstand a beating yet believe he can whip that same team next time. The list is endless of great athletes who have been soundly defeated yet

Starting stance—both feet must be firmly on ground and in contact with rubber.

returned to overcome their opponents. Even the finest fast-pitch pitchers have been beaten by a supposedly inferior team. Some of the all-time greats in the major leagues have had a disastrous season only to become a leading pitcher the following year.

A pitcher lacking confidence will have an adverse effect on his teammates. Coaches must stress this to aspiring youngsters who experience a lack of self-confidence. A good coach will also encourage teammates to praise the pitcher when he or she performs well. It's also important that teammates do not get down on the pitcher when he or she has a bad game. This is essential during the formative years. The pitcher who has his teammates' support and believes in himself has a head start toward becoming a leading hurler in the game of fast pitch.

BASIC TECHNIQUES

Teaching the young pitcher how to assume the proper stance on the mound should be the first step in his learning process. Although it is the most basic fundamental, it is even violated by experienced throwers. Both feet should be planted firmly on the ground, in contact with the pitching rubber. Neither foot can be placed at the side of the rubber.

Prior to any motion of the pitching delivery the pitcher must come to a complete stop and face the batter. His or her shoulders should be in line with first and third base. The ball must be held in both hands in front of the body. This position has to be maintained for at least one second but not more than twenty seconds.

After the pitcher holds the pause position for one second, he or she then begins the pitching motion. As soon as one hand is removed from the ball or any motion of the windup is started, the regulation pitch begins.

DELIVERY

During the delivery, the pitcher is allowed only one stride which must be toward the hitter.

Pause position must be held for at least one second.

The rear foot (pivot foot) must stay on the rubber until the ball is released. Foot faults are the most common mistakes made by fast-pitch pitchers. One of the most common faults is the "crow hop." This occurs when the pitcher takes a small jump off the rubber during delivery, the rear foot coming off the rubber before the ball is released. Another common error is moving the front foot forward and off the rubber before the delivery begins. Rocking backward with the rear foot off the rubber to gain momentum is another.

Foot faults often originate when the pitcher starts his or her career. Coaches should watch for those errors and correct them immediately. Otherwise the fault becomes a part of the pitcher's delivery and will be extremely difficult to correct later. It is not uncommon for a pitcher to pick up a bad habit and pitch for years before the fault is detected. Unfortunately, the error is often discovered at the high point of the pitcher's career. Sometimes, the effectiveness of the hurler is drastically reduced when trying to conform to pitching regulations.

LEGAL DELIVERY

A pitch must be delivered with an underhand motion. Both the release of the ball and follow-through of the hand and wrist must be forward and past the straight line of the body. The hand must be below the hip and the wrist no farther from the body than the elbow as the arm passes the straight line of the body. A baseball "submarine" or sidearm delivery is not allowed.

This definition must be understood by coaches. When the youngster is ready to throw stuff, there is a fine line between a legal and an illegal delivery. It should be noted that the rule does not forbid the wrist and hand from being outside the elbow just before passing the straight line of the body. Actually an extension of the wrist and hand beyond the elbow is the means by which rotation or "stuff" is generated. However, the wrist may be extended only prior to passing the straight line of the body but not as it passes that line.

Admittedly there is a small contradiction between a strict interpretation of a legal delivery and the real world of pitching. For example, the rule states that the release and follow-through of the hand and wrist must be forward. However, there is no way to throw a rise ball, particularly a curve, without turning the wrist slightly. Nevertheless, this contradiction has not amounted to much of a controversy among umpires.

WINDUP

There are several restrictions a young pitcher must consider in developing a windup. First, no movement can be made without delivering the ball immediately. That means there can be no hesitation, stopping, reverse motion, or fake movement.

The rules state that a rocker movement is not permitted. A rocker motion consists of the fol-

Hand must be below hip and wrist no farther from the body than the elbow as arm passes straight line of body.

Wrist may be extended only prior to passing straight line of the body.

lowing routine: After assuming the pause position, the pitcher takes one hand off the ball, makes a backward, then forward, swing, then returns the ball to both hands in front of the body. Also, only one complete arm revolution can be made.

Today, two basic styles are used: The slingshot and the windmill. Although controversy exists as to which style is best, the windmill has become the most popular in recent years. However, during the forties and fifties the slingshot was the most popular style of outstanding pitchers.

Whether one throws the windmill or the slingshot, the motion and coordination of the pitch is similar to an overhand pitch in baseball. The pitch is a definite throwing action, not like that used in bowling or pitching horseshoes. An underhand fast-pitch hurler employs the shoulder, upper arm, lower arm, and wrist. This type of throwing motion employs a full-run type snap that must be executed through one fluid motion.

SLINGSHOT

When using the slingshot delivery the arm is brought back slow, then snapped forward. The following description of how to take a position on the rubber is typical of most hurlers. However, some pitchers use slightly different approaches during the delivery. A right-handed pitcher places his or her right foot a short distance in front of the left foot. The toe portion of the right shoe is placed slightly in front of the rubber with the heel making contact with the rubber. Normally, the left foot is positioned about four to five inches behind the right foot. The toe position of the left foot makes contact with the rear portion of the rubber. The stance is reversed for a left-handed pitcher. Placement of the rear foot varies between pitchers. Some place the rear foot directly behind the front, while some spread the feet. Foot placement on the slingshot is the same as for the windmill.

Prior to delivery, always assume the official pitching position. The first move consists of

1. Start of backswing for slingshot motion.

2. Wrist cocked just prior to passing hip.

Slingshot Sequence

3. Arm straight and wrist even with elbow at point of release.

4. Final follow-through of slingshot motion.

WINDMILL

Pitchers using the windmill delivery have their own variation. Nevertheless, there are two prevailing basic styles. The customary delivery begins when the chucker assumes the official pitching position. As the ball is taken out of the glove, the upper portion of the body bends slightly forward, knees bent slightly in preparation for the stride forward. The pitching arm is raised above the head and continues in a circular motion. Although it is hard to detect without photos or a slow-motion camera, the arm bends at the elbow at the top point of the delivery. At this point, the wrist is slightly cocked. Bending of the arm and cocking of the wrist provide speed as well as generating stuff. The stride forward is continued simultaneously with the circular arm motion.

When the ball is released, the forward foot is firmly planted. The arm continues on its follow-through and the rear foot then comes off the rubber.

While a few may leave the rear foot against the rubber after release, most lift the rear foot almost simultaneously with the release of the ball.

WINDMILL-PUMP

A pump motion is also used with the windmill delivery. Rather than taking the pitching hand from the glove at the start of the windup, the hurler lifts both arms toward his chest. In some instances the hands are brought behind the head. The arms are then moved downward as the ball is taken out of the glove and the pitcher begins the windmill delivery. Most pitchers who prefer the pump motion claim that it provides them with extra momentum and a constant rhythm.

PITCHING RUBBER

Although the young pitcher can practice almost anywhere, he or she should throw from a regular pitching rubber whenever possible. The pitching plate should be made of wood or rubber and be twenty-four inches long and six inches wide.

There is no mound in softball as in baseball,

removing the ball from the glove. The pitching arm is then moved in a downward and backward motion. This movement continues until the pitching hand is behind and above the head. As the ball is drawn from the glove, the pitcher leans forward, knees bent, and starts the forward stride. The front leg is fully extended when the pitching arm is at the farthest point of the backward swing. At this point, the pitching arm is snapped forward and the front foot is planted firmly on the ground immediately prior to releasing the ball.

and the top of the pitcher's rubber must be level with the ground.

A young pitcher will have more success if he or she always throws to an official home plate, a five-sided figure. An official plate is 17 inches across the portion facing the pitcher. Both sides of the plate should be parallel to the inside lines of the batter's box and measure 8½ inches wide. Sides of the point facing the catcher should be 12 inches long.

The official pitching distance for men is forty-six feet, for women forty feet. But female slow pitch is forty-six feet.

It is imperative that the young pitcher develop a smooth motion and windup that is comfortable. Coaches need not be too concerned about control or speed in the early stages of learning. The delivery and windup should be repeated until every move feels natural. Excessive concentration on speed or control may impede progress. As the rookie becomes comfortable with the delivery, it will become easier to throw strikes as well as increase velocity.

Windmill Sequence

3. Beginning of circular motion.

2. Start of windmill delivery.

1. Presentation position.

4. Arm bent at top of motion.

5. Downswing of delivery.

7. Release and follow-through of windmill delivery.

6. Wrist cocked prior to passing hip.

FOLLOW-THROUGH

The follow-through is often taken for granted, yet it is a key part of the delivery. Correcting poor follow-through early prevents difficulties later.

Once the ball leaves the pitching hand the arm swing should continue in a smooth upward motion. But each pitcher will eventually develop his or her own preference for the final height of the arm swing. A continuous arm motion results in better control and more velocity.

Proper placement of the striding foot is another prime consideration. The striding foot should be placed in the same spot each time the ball is released. At the time the foot is placed, the toes should be pointed at home plate. This foot position permits good balance, aids control, and allows the pitcher to be in good fielding position. After the ball is released, the pivot foot is brought forward, even and parallel with

Striding foot should be pointed straight forward.

the front foot. Then a slightly crouched position with legs spread and weight on the balls of the feet should be taken. In this position the pitcher can move in any direction without stumbling, reacting to ground balls, line drives, even bunts.

Coaches can check consistency of foot placement by placing sand or lime at the approximate point of the finished stride. Often pitchers end their stride with the feet at awkward angles instead of pointing straight.

FIELDING

Many fast-pitch pitchers are inferior fielders. A good fielding pitcher is an asset, so teaching fielding skills is just as necessary as working with the youngster on delivery. Once the young pitcher learns the importance as well as the techniques of good fielding, he or she will retain them.

As pitchers mature it is common for them to neglect fielding. Consequently, it is often the responsibility of the coach to overcome this problem. It is a good idea to play young pitchers at other positions, frequently including them in infield drills.

PLAYING THE BUNT

Substantial time should be devoted to teaching the rookie how to handle the bunt. Defensing the bunt requires split timing and intricate moves. In practically every bunt situation the pitcher must throw to the fielder while running toward the base. The pitcher is actually trying to hit a moving target. It's advantageous to work on this move until the young hurler feels comfortable in a variety of sacrifice bunt situations.

Coaches can hurry the learning process by simulating game conditions. Have a hitter drop a sacrifice bunt just as it would happen in a regular game. To get the runner, the pitcher must quickly charge the bunt. A word of caution is necessary, however. A pitcher should not charge too fast or he or she may not be able to change direction if the ball takes a bad hop.

The bunt should be charged with feet spread. Gently scoop the ball into the glove, immediately grasping it. This step should be repeated often without throwing the ball. Get the player

Pitcher charges bunt with feet well spread.

in the habit of being sure he or she has a firm grip before throwing. Looking up before gripping the ball causes many errors.

Once the pitcher has made a definite play for the bunt, the catcher will shout which base to throw the ball. Whether it's another infielder or the pitcher, it's the catcher's responsibility to call the play. By practicing this maneuver again and again, the pitcher will become accustomed to listening for the catcher's instruction. There are occasions when the catcher's view is blocked and he cannot make the call. The pitcher must then make his own decision. Usually it's best to throw to first in this instance.

BACKING UP BASES

Backing up the proper base is another responsibility of the pitcher that is not given adequate attention by coaches. If a coach works with pitchers on this move, they will react automatically when the occasion arises. A pitcher who performs this move well takes considerable pressure off the other infielders. Failure to back up third base, for example, could mean losing a key contest.

SLOW PITCH

From a technical standpoint, slow-pitch pitching is much less complex. The slow-pitch hurler does not need to learn to throw curves, drops, rise balls. For all practical purposes, he or she needs to develop only one type of pitch, a high arching and slowly pitched ball. It should be noted, however, that there is a substantial amount of expertise required in delivering this pitch. Too many coaches underestimate the significance of the pitching position and the perfecting of a good slow-pitch delivery.

Rules require the pitcher to start the official pitch by taking the following position. One foot must be placed firmly on the ground, in contact with the pitching rubber. This foot may be touching any part of the rubber but not on the side.

Before any other move is made, the arm comes to a stop, holding the ball in front of the body with the pivot foot touching the rubber. This position should be held at least one second and not more than twenty before beginning delivery.

Every pitch must be thrown toward home

In slow pitch the arm remains straight. Wrist and elbow are not cocked as in fast pitch.

plate on the first forward swing of the pitching arm as it moves past the hip.

A legal pitch must be delivered underhand, and the arm should pass below the hip. Any motion that is part of the windup constitutes the start of the pitch. No halting or reversal of the forward motion is allowed. The pivot foot must remain touching the rubber until the ball is released. No restriction is placed on the placement of the front foot. However, if a step is taken, it must be made simultaneously with the release of the ball.

Each pitch must be thrown with a minimum detectable arc of three feet from the point of release until it crosses home plate. There is a limit of twelve feet on the highest point of the pitch.

All pitches must be moderate speed. Limitation on speed is up to the umpire. When an umpire feels the ball is being pitched too fast, he or she will give the pitcher a warning. If a fast pitch is repeated, the umpire will remove the

pitcher from that position for the remainder of the game.

RESTRICTION

Tape or other foreign substances must not be worn or attached to the pitching hand. Powdered resin may be used. However, the pitcher is not permitted to put resin directly onto the ball. Furthermore, the pitcher cannot wear a sweatband or jewelry on the hand, wrist, or forearm of the pitching arm.

"No Pitch" will be called by the umpire in the following situations: (1) If the pitcher pitches during suspension of play; (2) When the runner is called out for leaving the base too soon; (3) When the ball slips from the pitcher's hand during the windup or backswing. In all cases, the umpire will call the ball dead and all action following that pitch will be cancelled.

If the hurler fails to comply with the official pitching position, an additional ball is awarded the batter.

After each pitch the catcher must return the ball to the pitcher except after a strikeout or a putout made by the catcher. Also, the catcher must remain inside the catcher's box until the ball leaves the pitcher's hands.

An illegal pitch will be called by the umpire when a pitcher throws to a base while his or her foot is in contact with the pitching rubber. An illegal pitch will also be called if the pitcher fails to comply with any official pitching rule. When the illegal pitch is called, the umpire calls that pitch a ball, and the ball is dead. However, if the batter swings and misses an illegal pitch, it is considered a strike and no penalty is called against the pitcher. Furthermore, no penalty is called if the batter hits an illegal pitch. It should also be noted that baserunners do not advance on an illegal pitch as they do in fast pitch.

BASICS IN BEGINNING

Teaching basic rules and pitching regulations should be the first job of the coach. Obviously, throwing technique is the important aspect of pitching. Nevertheless, the inexperienced player should know the basic pitching position and the rules that govern that position.

Once the young hurler learns the fundamentals, he or she is ready to move to more advanced techniques. Knowing these fundamentals well is important to building self-confidence. Even the most talented youngsters feel uncomfortable when they make a mistake, particularly if the other members of the team are aware of it. Therefore, a well-coached individual has a good start in reaching his or her objectives.

4

Pitching—Advanced Techniques

Regardless of how well young pitchers respond to coaching, their success depends on their willingness to work hard. One of the best ways to work on control is through hours of regular practice with a catcher, preferably a good one. A catcher who prompts the hurler on what he or she is doing right or wrong is a great asset.

Good control demands that a pitcher execute the windup, delivery, and pitch consistently. A catcher can observe inconsistencies and call them to the pitcher's attention. Coaches should show catchers how to give the pitcher a clear target. During practice, the pitcher should concentrate on the given target area.

Another common practice is for the pitcher to call out where he or she is going to throw each pitch: high inside, low outside, etc. By repeating this routine many times, the hurler's control will improve more rapidly than throwing indiscriminately to home plate.

Whenever possible, the pitcher should use a batter in the box. Although this sounds strange, some pitchers can throw strikes all day until a batter steps up. Many have trouble throwing to a left-handed hitter, for example, yet are comfortable throwing to a right-hander. If a batter is not available, putting a chair in the batter's place can substitute.

Footwork is another area to work on. Stepping too far right or left can affect the delivery. The length of the forward stride should also be considered. Occasionally, a pitcher will unconsciously take an extra long stride, particularly when he or she tries to put something extra on a pitch. But quite often, the long stride throws off timing.

With proper coaching and practice, control will almost become second nature. When a pitcher frequently worries about control, there's usually a deficiency that's been overlooked. In some instances, poor control is simply a lack of

Whenever possible, pitcher should use a batter during practice.

experience. The solution to that is obvious.

There are few experienced pitchers who persistently lose control. Often the answer to this problem is complicated. It could be due to a mental state, lack of concentration or self-confidence. Or it may be improper execution or bad timing. It could also be a combination of mental pressure and basic fundamental mistakes.

If a pitcher displays periods of wildness, try to establish what happened just prior to the wildness. Maybe an error or an umpire's call disturbed the chucker. See if a pattern develops. Also, check if a pitcher has more trouble with a certain batting stance or position. Some pitchers knowingly have trouble throwing to a batter who stands deep in the box. Others have difficulty with hitters who crowd the plate. Once the problem is isolated, corrective measures can be taken.

It is not uncommon for a pitcher to have a wild streak after a couple of solid hits. At that point, he or she is told to bear down. As a result, the pitcher tries to throw too hard and deviates from his or her normal windup and delivery. A good coach sees these inconsistencies and immediately makes corrections.

TIPS FOR CONTROL

1. Before each pitch concentrate on the exact spot you wish to throw.
2. Always throw to a regulation plate in practice. Try to hit corners.
3. Be sure the lead foot lands in the same spot on every pitch.
4. When your pitches are consistently going inside or outside, move the pivot foot until you compensate for lack of control.
5. Scratch a line in the dirt from your pivot foot toward home plate. If you are right-handed, the left foot should land slightly left of the line.
6. Throw naturally and maintain good velocity on all pitches. Don't aim the ball.

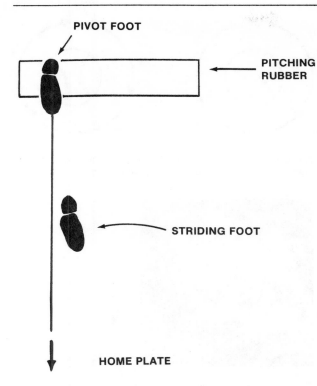

PIVOT FOOT

PITCHING RUBBER

STRIDING FOOT

HOME PLATE

Scratch line in dirt from pivot foot toward home plate. Left foot should land slightly left of line (right-hander).

7. Always bend the pivot knee slightly. This allows better push off.
8. Before every game, check the wind direction. When the wind is behind you, your pitches will break less but move faster. With wind blowing toward you, pitches break better and earlier.

TYPES OF PITCHES

When do you start teaching the young hurler how to throw stuff? As soon as possible. There has been much talk about youngsters throwing curves and rise balls when they are too young. If the pitcher is properly warmed up and has proper instruction, he or she is not likely to injure the throwing arm. Keep in mind that infielders, outfielders, and catchers can hurt their arms throwing a fastball just as easily as a pitcher throwing stuff.

In fast pitch, outstanding pitchers rarely throw a plain fast ball as in baseball. Virtually every pitch has something on it. The most com-

mon pitches are the drop, rise ball, curve, and change-up. A few throw excellent curve balls, however.

Probably the most important point to stress to young pitchers is that a ball breaks due to its rotation, not because of a certain grip. How much the ball breaks depends on the speed of rotation and the velocity of the pitch. The more the ball spins and the faster it is thrown, the more it breaks.

Drop

A drop ball in fast pitch is thrown very similarly to a fast ball in baseball. It is thrown by letting the ball roll off the ends of the fingertips. For best results, the drop should have a straight downward spin.

Drop is thrown most effectively by letting ball roll off ends of fingertips.

The drop is released with the palm of the hand pointed downward and parallel to home plate. On the follow-through, the palm comes up facing skyward. In most cases, the ball is gripped with the fingers across the seams. A majority of pitchers prefer to grip the drop with two fingers, however, some use three or four.

To obtain a downward spin, the wrist should be snapped but not twisted. If the wrist is twisted, the ball will spin slightly sideways and downward. This reduces the effectiveness of the drop. It should be mentioned at this point that some pitchers throw a drop by completely turning the wrist over. Although the drop can be thrown well this way by a few, it is difficult for the average chucker to learn.

When thrown at the proper spot, a drop is probably the most effective pitch. A pitcher who consistently keeps the drop between about three inches below to about six inches above the knee is difficult to beat. Of course, any pitch below the knees is a ball, yet it is hard for a hitter to judge a ball when the pitch comes in a couple of inches below the knees.

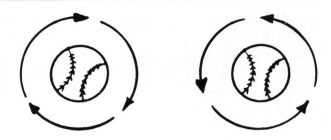

Viewing pitch from above, in-shoot spin is clockwise for right-hander, counterclockwise for left-hander.

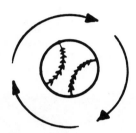

Viewing pitch from third-base foul line, spin of drop is clockwise.

A low drop is an excellent pitch for two reasons. First, it requires almost a golf-type swing to get at it. Secondly, the hitter usually hits on top of the ball, making it difficult to hit the low drop out of the park.

Keep in mind that the spin is toward home plate. To better visualize this spin, think of it this way: if you were standing on the third-base foul line, the spin would be clockwise.

In-shoot

An in-shoot or screwball is thrown and gripped much like the drop. The main difference is the release. Instead of straight downward spin, the ball will have a side spin. If one was able to look down on the ball from a platform, the ball would be spinning clockwise for a right-handed pitcher and counterclockwise for a left-hander.

Without question, the in-shoot is the most difficult pitch to master. Although it is effective, most pitchers have trouble throwing strikes consistently using the in-shoot.

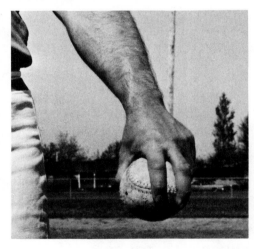

Various grips for throwing drop and in-shoot.

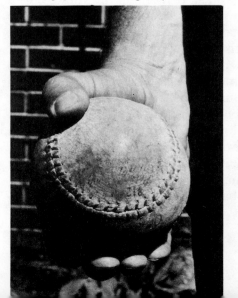

Ball comes off side of fingers on rise and curve.

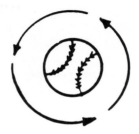

Pitch from third-base foul line, spin for rise is counterclockwise.

Rise

Just as the drop is thrown like a fast ball in baseball, the rise is thrown much like a baseball curve. Besides climbing steadily, a good sharp rise ball will hop or jump about the time it reaches the plate.

Many grips are used for the rise ball, one of the most common is the tucked finger method. One finger, usually the index finger, is tucked or bent, resting against a seam.

As the arm is brought forward on the downward swing, the wrist is cocked. This means that the hand is cupped, the wrist bent, extended outward beyond the forearm. The wrist is then turned (snapped quickly) immediately prior to passing the leg. At this point, the hand, wrist, and forearm become a straight line as the pivot leg is passed.

On the follow-through, the wrist continues to rotate. This combined action of the forearm and wrist causes the ball to have a backspin.

For obtaining the optimum rise the spin should be a straight backspin. If one stood on the third base side and could detect the spin, it would be a counterclockwise rotation. When a pitcher fails to get backspin, the rotation will be a corkscrew movement and the rise will tail off and not hop as it should.

Try to keep the rise ball from four to six

inches below the armpits to a couple of inches above. Pitches thrown above the armpits are out of the strike zone, but a good rise ball that breaks at the shoulders appears to be headed for the strike zone. This is a good spot to throw when the pitcher is ahead of the batter.

Although it's hard to perfect, the low rise is effective. The low rise looks like a drop to most hitters, and they tend to take the pitch. This pitch must be released early, and all the power comes from the forearm and wrist. The low rise should be thrown just above the knees.

Curve Ball

A curve is meant to move away from the batter. In other words, the right-handed thrower moves the ball away from a right-handed hitter. But when throwing to a left-handed hitter, the ball will break in. In most cases, a right-handed pitcher is less effective with the curve when throwing to left-handed batters.

To visualize the rotation of the ball, the curve from a right-handed pitcher moves counterclockwise when viewing the ball from above. The pitcher uses the curve in two ways. It can be thrown directly at the batter so it will back him or her up and then break across the plate. Another idea is to throw the curve toward the center of the plate and break it away to the outside corner.

When a right-hander is throwing to a left-hander, two different tactics can be used. First, the pitcher attempts to throw the ball to the outside corner of the plate so it appears to be a ball. The curve then breaks across the plate, and the hitter normally takes the pitch. A second method is to throw the curve so it seems to be

Various grips for throwing rise and curve.

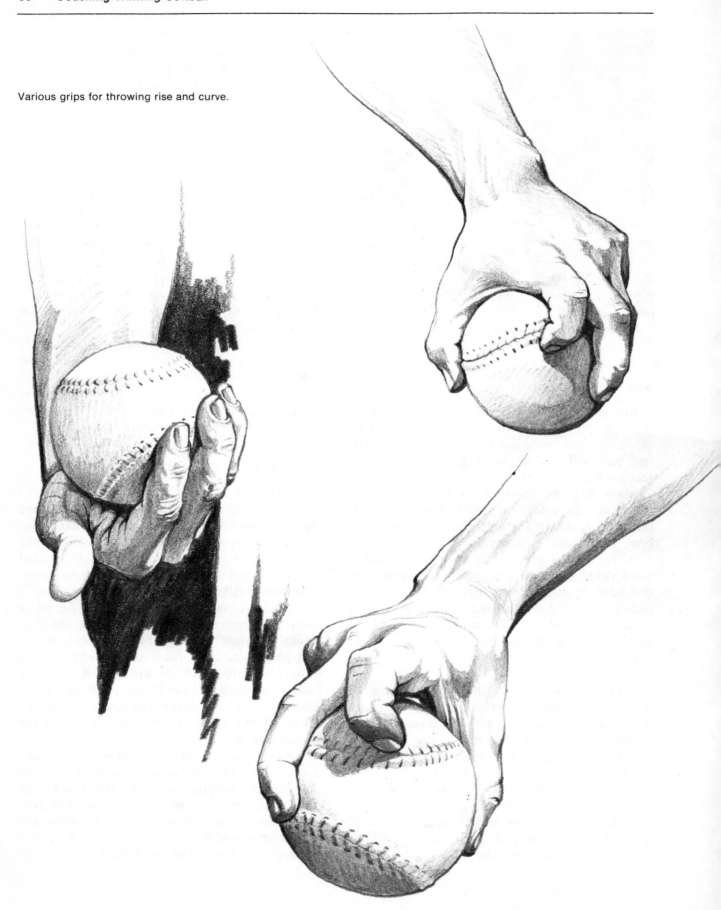

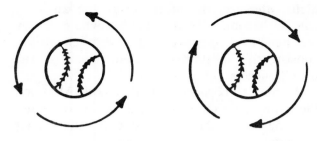

Viewing pitch from above, spin for curve is counterclockwise for right-handed pitcher, clockwise for left-handed pitcher.

coming across the heart of the plate, then breaks to the inside corner. When the hitter swings, the ball is usually hit near the wrists, so the batter seldom gets good wood. Remember, this explanation of the curve is theoretical. To execute the curve properly takes years of practice.

Most leading pitchers prefer the rise over the curve. A curve moves primarily in one plane, and if a pitcher grooves one across the heart of the plate, it's usually hit more solidly than the rise ball which is always climbing. A rise curve pitch is used successfully by many pitchers. This pitch is a combination of the curve and rise ball and is excellent for the pitcher's repertoire.

Change-up

Many pitchers go through an entire career and never develop a good change of pace. The trick to the change-up is to develop a consistent motion. Your delivery and release must appear to the batter to have the same motion of your other pitches. The pitcher must slow the velocity of the pitch without changing the speed of the regular windup and delivery motions.

The purpose of the change of pace is to confuse the hitter's timing. When a hitter is aware that a pitcher has a good change-up, he cannot dig in and take a full swing on every pitch.

When a mediocre pitcher develops a good change, he or she becomes good. When a good pitcher learns a change, he or she becomes outstanding. The change of pace may be a slow drop, a slow rise, or a slow curve.

Change-up Drop

A change-up drop is usually released just like the fast drop. The ball rolls off the ends of the fingertips. A major difference between the fast and slow drop is the wrist action. When throwing the fast drop the wrist is snapped, but on the slow drop the forearm and wrist are kept more rigid. The ball is more or less pushed out of the hand rather than thrown.

The change-up drop is more effective when kept low. Otherwise the hitter can pick it up easier. Also, when the change is delivered high, the batter will hesitate on his or her swing since it appears to be above the strike zone. This moment of hesitation gives the batter time to adjust the swing and a chance to connect squarely.

A few pitchers have some success throwing the change-up high. If the ball is delivered with considerable spin, it appears to be a high rise and the hitter often lets it drop for a called strike. Each pitcher learns through experience where he or she places the change-up most successfully.

Change-up Curve

When properly thrown, the change-up curve is one of the best pitches in the game. It keeps the hitter off stride and is a good breaking pitch.

Learning to throw the change-up curve requires concentration on snapping the wrist at the proper time. Rotation of the slow curve is faster than the regular curve. The best way to achieve this type of rotation is to place maximum effort on snapping the wrist, minimum effort on follow-through. In fact, the follow-through is practically eliminated. Some pitchers almost stop their delivery right at the hip.

Just like the regular curve, the slow curve can be used in two different ways. It can be thrown inside and then break across the plate. This technique is used to get the hitter to take the pitch for a called strike. The other way is to throw to the outside corner and break it outside. This method is effective because the batter is usually ahead of the pitch and cannot reach it even if he or she does time it fairly well.

Knuckle Ball

Virtually none of the great pitchers in softball have used the knuckle ball as a regular pitch. In fact, it is not advisable for coaches to spend much time teaching this pitch, even though it has been used successfully in major league baseball.

The size of the twelve-inch ball makes it difficult to properly hold a good-breaking knuckler. As a result, most pitchers who do employ the knuckle ball find they cannot throw this pitch consistently. The pitch must be released in a way which prevents the ball from spinning. A knuckle ball depends on wind currents to make it break rather than rotation and velocity. Since wind currents are affected by atmospheric changes, a knuckle ball may break well one day, yet another time it may be unpredictable.

The Fine Points

When teaching pitchers to throw curves, drops, in-shoots, rises, etc., remind them of the following points. A drop or in-shoot is thrown by letting the ball roll off the tips of the fingers. The curve and rise balls are thrown by letting the ball roll off the sides of the fingers.

Don't be too upset by a young pitcher's lack of control when he or she begins throwing stuff. Once the rookie has learned proper spin for each pitch, work at increasing his or her velocity. Control will improve with practice and game experience.

SLOW-PITCH

Without question, the fast-pitch pitcher is a dominating factor in softball. In slow pitch, the pitcher has little opportunity to dominate the game through pitching stuff. This statement should not be taken to mean that pitching skills are not important in slow pitch, however.

Since the pitcher is restricted from throwing fast, he or she must work on other pitching skills. The rules stipulate that the ball must have a minimum arc of three feet but cannot exceed twelve feet. Therefore, varying the arc is one factor influencing the angle of bat contact. The

higher the arc, the more severe the angle of contact becomes. Thus, a pitcher who can vary the height of the arc and still pitch strikes consistently substantially contributes to the team's success.

Pitching to corners is another skill. Although the batter has time to adjust the swing to corner pitching, he or she still must make the proper correction for hitting it squarely.

Slow-pitch hurlers can practice by themselves by placing a pail or basket on or just behind the plate and practice arcing the ball into the pail. The pail can be moved forward or backward as well as on the corners of the plate. Repeating this exercise frequently will sharpen the pitcher's ability.

PITCHING STATEGY

It is rare to find a hitter who has no batting weakness. The secret to becoming a great pitcher is to locate that weakness and take advantage of it. An alert coach will observe each hitter to discover differences.

One of the best aids for the pitching coach is a pitching chart. The pitching chart provides a record of what type of pitch was thrown and whether it was a ball or strike. When the batter hits it, the chart indicates if it was a line drive, a grounder, or a fly and where it was hit. When charting a game, the person keeping the record should consult with the catcher and pitcher after each inning. At this time, the pitches are fresh in their memory and they may provide special comments that should be recorded for future reference. Prior to a game, the coach, pitcher, and catcher should review the pitching charts. In the event you are playing a team for the first time, a new chart will be made. After each inning, it's a good idea for the coach, pitcher, and catcher to examine the chart. There should at least be a verbal discussion of the strengths and weaknesses of each hitter.

After establishing that a hitter is weak on a certain pitch, the coach encourages the pitcher and catcher to exploit this area. For example, a hitter may be weak on the rise ball but hits the daylights out of a drop. It is reasonable to throw the rise ball with greater frequency to this hitter. Nevertheless, it is not good strategy to throw it every pitch. A smart catcher and pitcher will mix up the routine to keep the hitter off balance.

Other factors enter into pitching strategy. Besides being weak on a certain pitch, hitters frequently have trouble with pitches thrown in a given area. Some batters prefer high outside rise balls, yet have trouble with high inside rises.

It's worth noting that there are hitters who can really belt the ball when it's thrown out of the strike zone. One very nationally known catcher liked to hit the rise ball at eye level. Teams not familiar with this catcher usually discovered this too late. Pitchers trying to waste a pitch by throwing it high often were surprised when he hit it out of the park.

STUDY HITTERS

When a hitter pulls, this means that he or she meets the ball well in front of the plate. To pull the ball, the batter usually swings early. Often this type of hitter is weak on a change-up. Drops, curves, or rises thrown to the outside corner are good choices for the pull hitter.

A hitter who consistently hits to the opposite field is meeting the ball at the rear of the plate. An inside drop or rise ball will be effective against the opposite-field hitter. This type of hitter is not fooled on the change-up as easily as the pull hitter.

If a batter prefers to stand in front of the batter's box, that batter probably believes he or she can get a good cut at the ball before it breaks. Even though this sounds reasonable, there is little evidence to support it. A good pitcher can often fool the up-front hitter with a high drop, a curve on the rear inside corner, or a low rise.

The hitter who chooses to stand deep in the box feels he or she has more time to look at the pitch. Be careful using the change-up on this hitter; keep it low. A low drop, a high outside curve, or rise should give this hitter the most trouble.

Hitters who crowd the plate or those who stand far away are often compensating for a weakness. For example, by standing far away from the plate, the hitter may be seeking protection against the low inside drop. A breaking curve or rise curve over the outside corner should be effective in this case. Again remember that your pitches need not all be outside. By occasionally challenging the hitter with an inside drop, he or she will be kept guessing.

A hitter crowding the plate bothers some pitchers. It seems to reduce the strike zone. As a result, plate crowders are often walked or hit. A hitter may be trying to protect the outside corner or may simply feel comfortable in this position. For the most part, the inside drop thrown low or the rise or curve pitched high and inside are most effective against hitters who crowd the plate.

The preceding tips are intended to be a starting point for the coach to work with. These suggestions will not be applicable to every hitter but should apply to the average situation faced by the pitcher. The more your team plays against any given team, the more familiar each pitcher becomes with opposing batter strengths and weaknesses. By the same token, the opposing hitters are aware of how your pitchers are throwing.

Once a smart hitter figures out the pitcher, that hitter looks for certain pitches on a given count or situation. Coaches should remind the pitcher not to develop a pattern. For example, a certain hitter may be weak on the rise. If the pitcher throws a rise on the first and second pitch and a low drop on the third, eventually the hitter will recognize this pattern and be prepared. Always mix it up.

WARM-UP

A warm-up period is mandatory. A warm-up period not only prepares one physically, but it provides time for getting ready mentally.

Jogging and wind sprints provide an ideal start for the warm-up period. This can be followed by calisthenics. Sit-ups, touching toes, and leg lifts loosen up a variety of muscles. Warm-up time depends on temperature, the pitcher's condition, and the time of the season. Early in the season, more time should be spent warming up.

PITCHING CHART

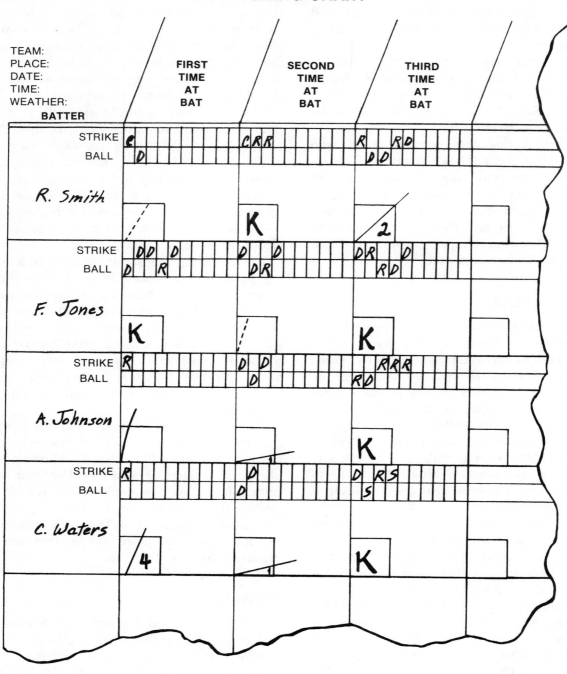

BATTER		FIRST TIME AT BAT		SECOND TIME AT BAT		THIRD TIME AT BAT	
R. Smith	STRIKE	C	CRR	R RD	
	BALL	D		DD	
			K	/2	
F. Jones	STRIKE	DD D	D D	DR D	
	BALL	D R	DR	RD	
		K		K	
A. Johnson	STRIKE	R	D D	RRR	
	BALL		D	RD	
				K	
C. Waters	STRIKE	R	D	D RS	
	BALL		D	S	
		/4		K	

CODE

D: DROP	1 SINGLE	——— LINE DRIVE
R: RISE	2 DOUBLE	⌒ FLY BALL
C: CURVE	3 TRIPLE	- - - - - GROUND BALL
S: CHANGE UP	4 HOME RUN	
I: INSHOOT	W WALK	
	K STRIKE OUT	
	HP HIT BY PITCH	

A jacket should be worn at the beginning, since the heat generated from exercising will aid in warming and loosening ligaments and muscles. This is particularly essential on a cool night.

Obviously, the throwing portion of the warm-up is critical. Begin throwing easy, both underhand and overhand. Then throw half-speed with a smooth underhand motion.

When all muscles feel loose and free, start the final portion of the warm-up routine. For best results, it is wise to throw at the regulation distance. Many fast-pitch hurlers prefer to warm up at distances substantially longer than the regulation forty-six feet. There is no benefit to this. If there was, major-league coaches would encourage baseball pitchers to do the same. In fact, warming up at long distance may be a disadvantage, since the hurler must adjust quickly early in the game.

Once the pitcher is ready to throw stuff, he or she should stick with one type of pitch. Start by pitching stuff at three-quarter speed, gradually increasing to full speed. Then switch to another pitch and follow the same routine until the repertoire is completed. Now the pitcher should mix the pitches similar to game conditions.

Coaches should encourage hurlers to use their regular windup, stride, and delivery during warm-up. Special attention must be given to footwork. Many fast-pitch hurlers take an extra step while warming up. This step is not allowed during a regular game. Undoubtedly it is the reason for early inning wildness.

TIPPING

Tipping pitches means that the hurler does something which permits the hitter or opposing base coach to predict what pitch is coming. After all, the purpose of learning to throw stuff is to fool the hitter. But if the pitcher gives the pitch away, the pitch is wasted.

A national championship may hinge on one pitcher's ability to hold the opposing team in check. There have been instances where a pitcher has thrown every game in a national tournament to help win the championship. This means that one pitcher carried the entire burden. However, there have been times when a

Hide grip by placing ball deep in glove.

pitcher has been virtually unbeatable during a season, yet during a few crucial games in a tournament he or she has been hit hard and often. Many fail to realize that the reason for this drastic turnaround is that opposing coaches discovered tipping.

There are many ways a pitcher can give pitches away. First of all, the pitcher may fail to hide his or her grip. If the pitcher is careless, the hitter may pick it up from the batter's box. Often the third- or first-base coach can see the grip, relaying the information to the hitter. It is relatively easy to correct this. A good coach can show the pitcher how to hide his or her grip in the glove hand.

A pitch may be easily tipped at the presentation stage of the windup. It is not uncommon for the inexperienced hurler to hold the glove in one plane for one pitch, in another plane for a different pitch. Even a slight variation in the tilt of the glove may give the pitch away. A few pitchers are so careless that they hold the glove in different positions. For example, they may hold the rise ball up close to the letters and place the glove near the belt for the drop.

When the pitcher removes the ball from the glove to begin the windup, he or she should vary the motion. Sometimes the hurler may drop the ball for a drop but bring it straight back toward his or her hip on the rise.

Variation in the movement on the pump motion occurring immediately after the presentation can also tip a pitch. Watch the position of the shoulders at the start of the delivery to see that they do not drop or raise on different pitches.

Coaches should review a pitcher's windup and delivery periodically to see if they have developed telltale movement. If possible, take moving pictures, since this is excellent for picking up variations in grip, presentation, and windup.

SLOW PITCH

Pitchers in slow pitch need not concern themselves with learning to throw stuff. Nevertheless, the material presented for fast pitch in this chapter is applicable to the slow-pitch hurler. Items such as the warm-up routine and recognizing hitters' weaknesses and strengths will be helpful to the slow-pitch chucker as well as the pitcher in fast pitch.

5

Catching

One characteristic befitting a catcher stands out above all—leadership. He or she should be a take-charge person who commands the respect of the team.

Particularly in fast pitch, the catcher is the controlling player in the game. He or she has the responsibility of calling pitches and directing throws on bunt situations.

Coaches too often overlook the importance of a catcher in relation to a pitcher's performance. A good catcher not only handles the pitcher's stuff proficiently, but should be capable of giving the pitcher a psychological lift. The catcher must be able to detect any change in the pitcher's stuff as well as in his attitude. Then he or she must quickly react to that change and offer constructive assistance.

Because the catcher calls the game for the pitcher, he or she is the one most familiar with how the batter handles each pitch. In addition to recorded statistics, the catcher must re-member each hitter's weaknesses and the pitcher's ability to cope. A catcher must have an excellent memory and be alert.

Catchers should not be distracted by an unexpected turn of events. Because catchers are to some degree involved in almost every play in the game, they have to be well acquainted with the rules of the game.

PHYSICAL ATTRIBUTES

Even though catchers come in all sizes, there are a few physical characteristics they should have. First, a catcher needs quick reactions. He or she does not have to be a sprinter, but must be able to move quickly.

It's an advantage for a catcher to have a strong build, but not necessary. The catcher is the player most likely to take hard bumps from runners trying to score.

A strong arm is a plus for the youngster

wishing to be a good catcher. This doesn't mean that a player who doesn't have a strong arm cannot catch. A player who can throw accurately and quickly has a good chance of becoming a fine catcher, providing he or she has other needed qualifications.

Quick hands are a must. The catcher has to be capable of quickly changing the position of the glove. Catchers must be ready for pitches in the dirt, high fast-breaking rise balls, and wide pitches.

Left foot is placed slightly ahead of right foot. Weight is distributed on balls of feet.

STANCE

The catcher is required to be in a relatively uncomfortable position while on the field. Therefore it is imperative to find a stance that is comfortable yet correct for receiving and throwing. The proper position is a combination of a crouch and squat, feet well spread.

Most catchers place the left foot slightly ahead of the right foot, their weight distributed on the balls of their feet. This position allows for maximum movement in any direction. It is also the best position for preparing to throw.

An experienced catcher gets as close to the batter as possible. In this spot, he or she can handle low pitches more effectively than standing several feet behind the hitter. Rookie catchers commonly position themselves several steps behind the hitter. Of course this causes the inexperienced player to have trouble with pitches that bounce in the dirt. The fear of standing close to the batter will be overcome by practice and game experience.

SIGNALS

Flashing signals to the pitcher seems simple and uncomplicated, yet signaling can be quite complex.

Signals are given while the catcher is squatting. Knees are spread and the sign is given with the throwing hand. The glove hangs over the left knee, hiding the signal from the opposing third-base coach.

Signals are given with fingers of bare hand placed in crotch area.

Signals are flashed with the fingers from the crotch area. Be sure that the rookie catcher does not flash signs with fingers held below the crotch, otherwise the opposing third- or first-base coach can easily steal the sign and relay it to the batter. In addition to keeping the fingers deep in the crotch area, a coach must watch for unusual movements that may give away the signal. A distinct movement of the wrist or elbow for a certain sign can be picked up.

Signals may be kept very simple when second base is unoccupied by a runner. For example, one finger designates the rise; two fingers, the drop; three fingers, a curve; four fingers, a change-up; etc. With second base occupied, the catcher and pitcher must use a more complex code. A common system consists of a key sign followed by a prearranged set of signals. The key sign indicates which signal will be the correct pitch wanted. For instance, if the catcher flashes two fingers first, this means the correct sign will be the second signal after the key sign. By using this system the signals can be varied for each hitter. With a little thought a coach can devise many codes to prevent runners from picking up the signs.

Place body in front of pitches in the dirt, fingers of glove pointed down.

RECEIVING

Once the catcher has flashed the signal, he or she assumes the receiving position. As previously mentioned, each catcher should adopt the stance most comfortable for him or her. Some catchers prefer to remain in a complete squat position, others use the combination crouch/squat.

Immediately prior to the windup, the catcher gives the pitcher a clear target with the glove. Coaches differ on what the catcher should do with the throwing hand. Some prefer the catcher to clinch the fingers and hold them adjacent to the glove. Yet others instruct the catcher to hold the throwing hand behind the back. In either case, the purpose is to protect the throwing hand from injuries caused by foul tips.

To be instilled early into the catcher's mind is how to receive the pitch. A high pitch is caught with the finger portion of the mitt pointing up. The finger portion is pointed down on low balls.

With runners on base the catcher's primary job is to keep them from advancing. Of course a runner can advance in many ways. Yet nothing is more demoralizing to a team than having runners steal bases on their catcher or advance on passed balls.

Pitches that bounce in the dirt are always trouble. As soon as the catcher suspects that the pitch may hit the dirt, he or she moves in front

Fingers of throwing hand should be clinched to prevent injury from foul tips.

Catcher should move toward infield to get better angle on throw to first.

of the ball. Some catchers prefer to drop to their knees in this situation. When you place your body in front of the low pitch the ball usually bounces back toward the playing field. This allows the catcher to see the ball and gives him or her a better opportunity to hold the runner on.

The tight inside pitch is particularly tough for the catcher to handle cleanly since the batter's body hides the ball. In this situation the catcher must attempt to move in front of the pitch rather than just reaching for the ball.

THROWING

Regardless of which base the catcher throws to in an attempt to get a runner, the important part of the throw is accuracy, not velocity. In nearly every instance, a catcher must get rid of the ball quickly whether it's on a bunt, a topped ground ball, or a steal.

An inexperienced catcher not only tries to throw too hard, but often is out of position. Therefore, the coach should emphasize accuracy and footwork when throwing to bases.

When an experienced catcher throws a runner out trying to steal, the footwork and throw appear to be one smooth movement. Nevertheless, this movement actually consists of several distinct moves coordinated into one fluid action.

The moment the ball leaves the pitcher's hands, the catcher must try to observe runner movement with his or her peripheral vision without losing sight of the pitch. If it appears the runner is going, the next step, maybe the most critical, is to make a clean catch. Any momentary bobble means the runner will be safe. Next, the ball is removed from the glove quickly, the arm cocks, and the left foot strides out. The final move is the throw. An ideal throw to second reaches the infielder slightly to the right of the bag (looking from home plate) and one to two feet above ground.

Coaches should work with catchers to get them to develop smooth footwork and throwing. Just throwing to second without the catcher actually receiving a pitch only accomplishes half the job. Practicing with a runner trying to steal is the ideal method.

INFIELD PLAYS

Fast pitch is demanding on the catcher. One of the most demanding is covering bunts. Here the catcher must get to the ball quickly without interfering with the hitter. After fielding the bunt, often requiring a bare-handed pickup, the throw is usually to the second baseman who is on the run to cover first. This throw is doubly difficult since the runner going to first has a tendency to distract the catcher.

Should the runner run inside the baseline, the rules state that the runner is out. Nevertheless, this is a difficult call for the umpire. Practicing this throw with a runner will vastly improve the catcher's ability to make this play.

If time permits, on a topped ground ball or bunt, the catcher should take an extra step toward the pitcher's mound after fielding the ball. This gives him or her a better angle to throw from, and the chance of missing the runner with the peg is substantially better.

The hitter running to first after a dropped third strike also presents a problem for the catcher. Since the ball usually ends up behind the plate, the throw has to be made from a bad angle. Sometimes the catcher has to make the throw from foul territory. Practicing this throw with a runner headed to first is helpful.

It should be noted that anytime the catcher makes a play on a fair ball he or she is moving to catch up with the ball. Therefore, the catcher seldom has time to field the ball like the rest of the infield. This is why it's good to practice bare-handed pickups which save time on close plays.

ANALYZE POSSIBILITIES

An experienced catcher tries to analyze the situation on every pitch. With a runner on first and a bunt a possibility, the catcher has several options if he or she fields the ball. First, a forceout at second is possible if the ball is retrieved quickly. In this instance, the shortstop will cover second, so the throw will be made to the third-base side of second. Otherwise, the peg may pull the fielder off the bag.

Second, the throw may have to go to first which will be covered by the second baseman.

Mask should not be thrown aside until pop fly is sighted.

In addition, the batter may pop up the bunt which will give the catcher a chance to make a double play. Sometimes the bunt will be so well placed that the catcher has little chance of making a play at any base. When this happens the catcher should hang on to the ball and not take a chance of throwing it away. Coaches should remind the rookie catcher to concentrate on every pitch and think ahead before making a play.

Wind direction is another consideration, particularly when the catcher must contend with a high pop-up. Whenever possible the catcher lets an infielder handle the pop-up. It's a lot easier to keep the ball in front of the body when the wind direction is known. Otherwise the catcher may have to backpedal to make the catch.

As soon as the catcher realizes the ball is popped up in foul territory, the mask is quickly

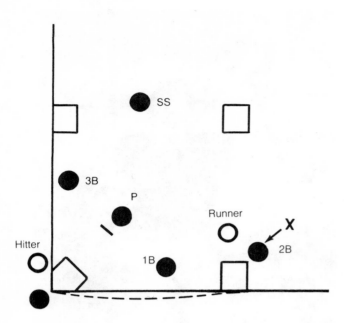

Second baseman moves in behind runner on the pick-off play.

taken off, but not thrown aside until the ball is sighted. Otherwise the mask might be tripped over as the catcher pursues the ball.

PICK-OFF

Few teams use the pick-off play successfully in fast pitch. Yet this play can give the defensive team a mental lift, completely demoralizing the opponent. The catcher plays the key role on this play in fast pitch. Since the runners cannot lead off, the pitcher plays only a minor role.

A bunt situation with a runner on first offers the optimum chance for the pick-off play. In this case, the runner on first tries to get a jump toward second after the pitcher releases the ball. When the catcher notices the runner getting a little careless, he or she calls for a pitch-out and flashes the pick-off signal. This signal must be obvious enough that the shortstop and second baseman can recognize it. As soon as the pitcher releases the ball, the first baseman charges in as if to field the possible bunt. At the same time, the second baseman sneaks in behind the runner and takes the throw from the catcher at first. The shortstop covers second in the event the trapped runner heads for second, and the right fielder backs up first in case of an overthrow.

PROTECTING HOME

The catcher really earns the respect of his or her teammates when making a key putout at home. Any runner worth his or her salt will be giving everything on a play at the plate. Many times the catcher will receive a shot from a hard slide, intended to jar the ball loose.

Regardless of how a runner comes in to score, sliding or standing up, the catcher's job is to protect or block the plate. Blocking the plate means different things. When the catcher gets between the runner and the plate he or she obviously has blocked the plate. By the rules, the catcher must have possession of the ball to block the plate. A body block of the plate is dangerous, and the rookie catcher should be discouraged from using this method.

One of the safest and most effective ways of blocking the plate is to make a tag from a crouch, feet straddling the plate. The glove hand, ball tightly gripped, is extended well out in front of the plate and placed on the ground. Many inexperienced catchers prefer to hold the ball tightly in the glove by using the bare hand as an aid. Remember the tag will be effective only if the catcher makes a clean catch on the throw in.

Throws to the plate frequently arrive on the bounce. To make a clean catch, the catcher must watch the ball all the way into his or her glove. A common mistake made by inexperienced players is to take their eyes off the ball to peek at the runner. This moment usually results in a bobbled catch and a score.

SLOW PITCH

Because bunting and stealing are not permitted in slow pitch, the catcher does not require a strong arm.

But the slow-pitch catcher should be the team leader. Keeping track of the outs, placing the fielders, and putting pep into the team are all the catcher's job. Even more important, the slow-pitch catcher must protect home plate. In comparison to fast pitch, there are far more plays to be made at home plate. Therefore, the catcher should have good hands and be stout. This position is an excellent spot for a person capable of belting the home run consistently.

Straddle plate and get glove in front on plays at home.

6

Infield Play

Although there are differences between fast-pitch and slow-pitch infield strategies, infielders in both sports must be quick. In contrast to ninety-foot basepaths in baseball, the basepath distance in softball is sixty feet. With no lost motion, the softball infielder must field cleanly and throw quickly and accurately to get the runner with only average speed.

BE READY

An infielder has to be prepared to move quickly in any direction. To be set on each pitch, a comfortable stance should be used. There are several variations of the infield stance. A full crouch, hands extended toward the ground, is a typical stance. The semi-crouch, hands on knees, is also used. When using the stance with hands on knees, remember to drop the hands toward the ground as the pitcher starts the delivery.

This typical stance permits infielder to move quickly in any direction.

Feet should be well spread, weight equally distributed on each foot. It's smart to always watch the ball. Using this procedure, the fielder will be alert and ready to move.

FIELDING THE BALL

There are several basic moves indispensable to the apprentice infielder. When properly instilled in the rookie's mind, they will stick with him or her.

Keep your hands well in front of you, low and close to the ground. Grounders are fielded by lifting the glove from the ground up. It's faster to lift your hands than to put them down. The minute the infielder sees the ball coming in his or her direction, he or she gets the glove and throwing hand on the ground.

Exercise: Start the rookie out by hitting slow grounders directly at him or her. Instruct the fielder to get the glove down quickly along with the bare hand. The hands should be relaxed. Have the fingers of the glove touch the ground. Cup the glove slightly and let the ball roll in. Do not reach out or swipe at the ball. As soon as the ball touches the glove, the throwing hand grips the ball in a way that will allow for a quick throw.

Infielders have better success with sidearm throws.

When possible, get in front of the ball. Reaching for a grounder is risky. Getting in front of the grounder will keep it from going past the infielder, even if it takes a bad bounce. Sometimes it's impossible to get in front of the grounder, and the infielder must reach or make a dive at the ball to keep it from going into the outfield.

Play the grounder, don't let it play you. An inexperienced infielder moves toward the grounder rather than waiting for it. This fundamental is particularly important in the case of a slow-moving ball hugging the ground or a topped ball taking several bounces. Sometimes it's easier to field a ball by waiting rather than taking it on a short hop, but it also gives the runner a couple of extra steps.

Throw accurately, not hard. A strong throw is great but getting rid of the ball quickly and hitting your target consistently is more important than throwing with great velocity. This requires proper footwork as well as throwing technique. Poor throws can frequently be traced to improper pivoting and planting of the lead foot. Fast-pitch infielders will have better success throwing with a sidearm or three-quarter motion rather than a straight overhand.

Exercise: A coach places the infielder at his or her deepest spot normally played for a grounder. The ball is rolled on the ground about half speed. The infielder charges, picks up

Get in front of ball whenever possible. Reaching to either side is risky.

the ball, quickly fires it to first. Just as the infielder releases the ball, the coach rolls another ball. This routine is repeated until the infielder makes several quick and accurate throws. During the exercise, the coach should correct any mistakes. A common mistake is to throw quickly before having a firm grip on the ball. Taking the eyes off the ball is another common error.

Make the throw only when there is a good chance to get the runner. When you decide not to throw, it's a good idea to fake it anyhow. There is always the possibility another runner may try to take an extra base. Inevitably, when there is little chance to get the runner, the throw is hurried and often goes wild.

FIRST BASE (FAST PITCH)

The first baseman handles the ball more often than any of the other three infielders. He or she must have unusual ability to field low-thrown pickups. This position requires a person with excellent balance and good footwork. It's an advantage to be tall, but many great first basemen have been small. Either a right-handed or left-handed person can play the position. However, it is easier for the left-hander to make tags, as well as throws to second base.

If ball is thrown to the extreme left of bag, shift weight so right foot touches inside corner of first.

When throw comes directly to bag, left-hander keeps left foot on bag and stretches right leg.

One of the first things a coach should concentrate on is to prepare the first baseman on the proper way of taking throws from other infielders. Because the first baseman usually plays in front of the bag, he or she must turn, run, and be positioned to take the throw in seconds.

As soon as the ball is hit to another infielder, the first baseman breaks for the bag. After reaching the bag, the first baseman faces the person who fielded the ball and straddles the bag. In this position, the first baseman can shift quickly in case of a wide throw.

When the throw comes directly to the bag, the left-handed first baseman keeps the left foot in contact with the bag and stretches the right leg. A right-hander keeps the right foot on the bag and stretches the left leg.

If a ball is thrown to the extreme left of the bag, whether you are right- or left-handed, shift so the right foot touches the infield corner of the bag and extend the left foot. On a ball

On balls thrown to extreme right, first baseman touches outfield corner of bag with left foot.

thrown to the extreme right of the bag, shift so the left foot touches the outfield corner of the bag and extend your right foot.

When a throw comes in on a bounce, your hands should be moving toward you, glove open. Never swipe at the ball. High throws are taken with a short jump and an open glove. If time permits, on a high throw, the first baseman can step into foul territory. A right-handed first baseman keeps the right foot on the bag, and the left-hander keeps the left foot on the bag.

A ball to the left side of the bag creates a difficult play. Often the ball is thrown directly into the runner's path. When there is time, the first baseman steps off the bag and tags the runner.

Inexperienced players usually make the mistake of staying on the bag too long on a wide throw. When there is any question of whether or not the ball can be reached, the fielder should come off the bag and stop the throw rather than attempting to stretch and get the out.

Immediately after making the catch, the first baseman comes off the bag and gets in a position to throw. Always watch the other baserunners. Never look at the umpire to see what call was made. Jump off the bag, size up the situation, then look at the umpire if the play was close.

Playing Position

Fast pitch requires the first baseman to play in front of the bag most of the time. The nature of the game and the dimensions of the field make every batter a potential bunter. With no runners on base and less than two strikes on the hitter, the first baseman plays about eight to ten feet in front of the bag. After two strikes, he or she usually moves back a few steps.

Bunt

When first base is occupied and there are no outs, an obvious bunt situation exists. In this instance, the first baseman often moves in within fifteen feet of the hitter. Although this seems very close, it is unnecessary when a good bunt is executed. The catcher will call out the proper base once the bunt is down. If the catcher calls first base, the first baseman throws to the second baseman who covers first. When the first baseman fields the bunt and the play is at second, the shortstop covers second.

A good fast-pitch team tries to get the runner at second on a sacrifice bunt play. If a bunt is hit to the first or third baseman, there is a good chance that a double play may be completed. However, if the runner going to second is speedy and the bunt is well placed, it's best to take the out at first and be sure of getting at least one.

When both first and second are occupied, the first baseman faces a tough choice. To make a play at third, the first baseman must throw past the pitcher and hit the shortstop on the run as he or she moves to cover third. Unless the ball is bunted hard and directly to the first baseman, it's best to make the play at first. A wild throw at this point means at least one run, maybe two.

Hitting Away

With less than two outs and a runner on first, be alert for a possible double play. Although you may be pulled in close for a possible bunt, you can still make the double play if the runner hits away.

If the ball is hit to the first baseman, he or she fires the ball to the shortstop covering second. He or she must then get to first to take the throw from the shortstop. If the first baseman is drawn in too close to get back to the bag, the second baseman, assuming he or she is alert, will dash to cover first.

Don't forget that the double play can be made by the first baseman touching first, then throwing to second. However, the player going to second must be tagged since the runner is not forced at second. For example, the hitter in this case might be fast, the runner on first slow. As a result, the first baseman can touch base, then throw to second to get the slow man on a tag.

With one or two outs and no one on base, most first basemen stay closer to the bag. This allows them more time to field hard-hit grounders and line drives. Slow-moving grounders between first and second are taken by the first baseman, since he or she plays in closer than the second baseman. The second baseman always covers first, since there is not sufficient time for the pitcher to cover first in fast pitch.

FIRST BASE—SLOW PITCH

Much of what has been said about the fast-pitch first baseman also applies to the slow-pitch first baseman. Though there are exceptions. The slow-pitch first baseman plays even with or behind the bag since bunting is not permitted.

The chance of completing a double play is good in slow pitch. The runner may not leave the base until the ball crosses home. Consequently, the fielders have more time to complete the play.

Since there are more hits in slow pitch, the first baseman should be an excellent fielder and have a good arm. This is a spot for a big, hard-hitting player with good hands. But since he or she does not have to cover bunts, the first baseman need not be fast.

SECOND BASE—FAST PITCH

The person playing second in fast pitch is usually the most versatile member of the squad. He or she must be alert, quick, and have good hands and an accurate arm.

One of the main jobs is covering first on the bunt. Properly doing this task requires practice and game experience. In a close game with first occupied and no one out, the second baseman should be ready for a sacrifice bunt. The first thing to do is take a few steps closer to first. As soon as the batter squares to bunt, move a step or two closer to first, never taking your eyes off the hitter. Once the bunt is down, dash to first and prepare to take the throw. As soon as the second baseman takes the throw, he or she immediately comes off the bag to be sure the runner going to second doesn't have a chance at third. Never turn to check the umpire's call until you are sure other runners are not trying to advance.

Grounders and Fly Balls

Fielding a grounder hit to the extreme right of the second baseman is always a challenge. First, the second baseman has to get to the ball fast. After that there are several choices. If the ball carries him or her to a point where a play at first is practically impossible, no play should be made. In the event the fielder gets to the ball quickly, he or she places weight on the right foot and gets braced in a balanced position. From this instance, an overhand throw should be made.

A well-coordinated second baseman should be able to field the ball while running, jump, turn, and throw to first. This is a difficult maneuver, but it can be learned through practice and game experience.

When first is occupied and a ball is hit to the extreme right, the second baseman should always consider the play at second. Here, it is often possible to make the force-out by touching the bag without making a throw. If it's not possible to beat the runner to second base, then a throw to the shortstop covering second is a good choice. The throw should be underhand or sidearm, thrown easily and accurately. A hurried throw usually results in the runner making it to third, even home.

Several choices are available to the second baseman on a ball hit to his or her extreme left. He or she may be able to make the pickup and make the out by touching first. If the play carries the second baseman deep, he or she must often make a running backhand throw to the first baseman. When first base is occupied and the ball is hit to the second baseman's extreme left, do not attempt the play at second. Always take the sure out at first.

The second baseman must charge slow, chopped grounders to get the out. This means the infielder must often take the ball on the short hop. Waiting for the high bounce makes the play easier but the chance for getting the runner is poor.

Even major leaguers have difficulty making plays on the short hop. Learning to do it well requires years of practice. Special emphasis should be placed on fielding slow, bouncing ground balls. This play requires the fielder to run, field, and throw during one quick, smooth movement. Too often, grounders hit to fielders in practice are fast-moving, easily handled. Slowly, chopped grounders that must be charged are those that usually cause the infielder to make mistakes. Therefore, more time should be devoted to this type of play in practice.

Because the first baseman plays in close, the second baseman is required to take most of the pop flies behind first base. On any fly near second, the second baseman makes a try for the catch. However, once another player calls for the ball, the second baseman returns to second.

Pop flies headed for the outfield are usually difficult to handle by the infielder, since he or she must often make the catch over the shoulder. It's best that the outfielder make the catch if possible. But if the outfielder cannot get to the ball, the infielder must. This play is further complicated with runners on base. As soon as the second baseman makes the catch, he or she quickly prepares to throw back to the infield.

Prior to a game on a sunny day, all infielders should decide with the coach who will take a high pop fly in the infield. Regardless of how experienced the infielder may be, the sun can temporarily cause him or her to lose the ball. The infielder who has the angle on the ball with the least direct rays from the sun will have the best opportunity to make the play.

Making the Double Play

Several key elements are critical in making the double play. First, if the ball is hit to another fielder, the second baseman's first responsibility is to head toward the bag. A second key move is getting positioned to take the throw. Approach the bag with feet well spread, maintaining good balance. Then if the throw is to you, shift to the right and touch the bag with the left foot. When the throw is to your left, shift to your left and touch the bag with the right foot. An ideal throw reaches the fielder about one or two steps before he or she hits the bag.

When taking a throw keep both hands together because this makes it easier to get rid of the ball. If it is not possible to touch the bag,

On double play, shortstop steps past second with left foot and drags right foot across bag.

the recommended procedure is to take the throw before reaching the bag. Then step over it with your left foot and drag the right foot across it.

On a ball hit to the right of the second baseman, the throw is usually made with an underhand toss. When the ball is hit directly at the fielder or slightly to his or her left, the throw is made with a sidearm motion. In either case, the ball should hit the fielder waist- to chest-high.

Tags at Second

A second baseman usually covers the bag or the steal when a right-hander is at the plate. However, the second baseman may cover the bag when a left-hander is at bat, particularly if the hitter has a reputation for hitting to the opposite field. Experienced infielders always discuss the situation before the play takes place. It is important that the infielder inform the catcher as to who will cover on a steal.

To execute coverage, the second baseman must get a jump toward the base, doing this by watching the runner closely. The minute he or she detects the runner is going, he or she heads for the bag. Any pause means the runner will probably be safe. As the second baseman heads toward the bag, he or she should keep an eye out for the throw from the catcher rather than getting to the bag, then looking for it.

One of the most common mistakes made by an inexperienced player is to peek at the runner. Keep your eye on the throw and make a clean catch. After the catch, the tag should consist of

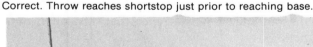

Correct. Throw reaches shortstop just prior to reaching base.

Wrong. Ball gets to second baseman too late.

one smooth motion. The surest way to make the tag for a beginner is to use both hands. A more experienced second baseman uses the glove hand only. The ball is clamped tightly, and the infielder allows the runner to slide into the back side of the glove. This way, the ball will not be easily dislodged.

Handling Relays

On a base hit to right or right center field, the second baseman quickly runs to short right field in case a relay throw is needed. In most cases the relay throw is required only on extra-base hits. The second baseman then takes the throw from the outfielder and relays it to either third base or home.

Since the second baseman has his or her back to the infield, the shortstop or first baseman normally calls out where the ball should be thrown. When the throw is long, it's best to throw a one-bounce peg to the third baseman or catcher covering the play. The relay throw should be made with an overhand motion rather than the sidearm motion normally used by the infielders.

SECOND BASE—SLOW PITCH

The slow-pitch second baseman plays deeper than the fast-pitch second baseman, not having to worry about covering first on bunts or second on steals. Playing deeper, the second baseman has a better opportunity to cut off potential ground ball or line-drive hits.

The slow-pitch second baseman should be fast, have exceptional hands, and the ability to get rid of the ball quickly. Further, he or she should be able to get back quickly on pop flies. This capability is necessary in slow pitch, since the outfielders play deeper than fast-pitch outfielders.

Baseball experts claim that a good team must be strong down the middle, second base and shortstop. This also applies to slow pitch. In order to be a contender in slow pitch, the second baseman and shortstop must be outstanding fielders.

Fundamentals covered for the fast-pitch second baseman also apply to the slow-pitch second sacker. A good second base-shortstop combination can complete key double plays, strengthening team effectiveness.

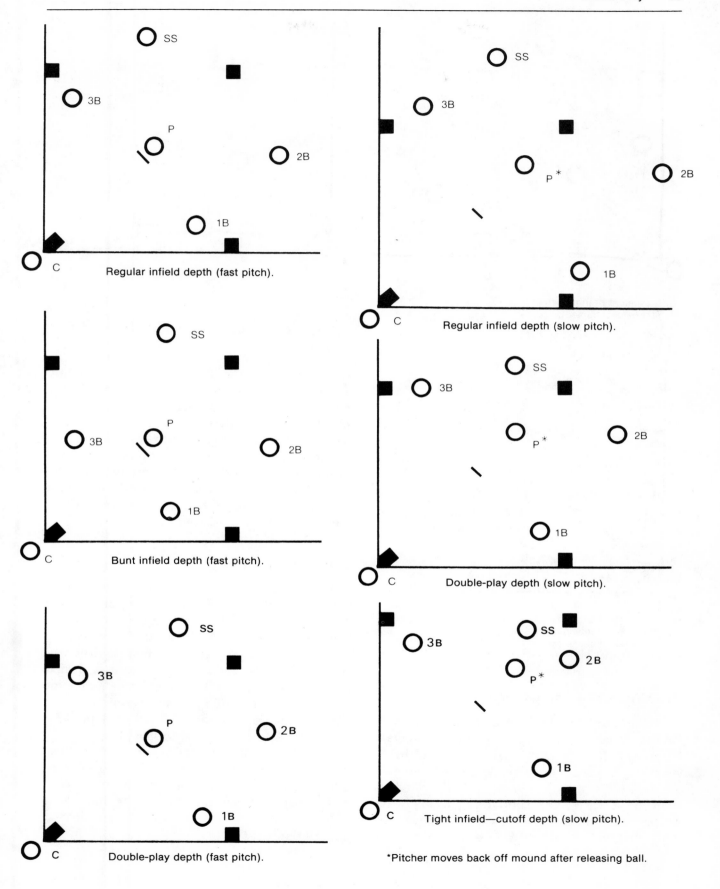

Regular infield depth (fast pitch).

Regular infield depth (slow pitch).

Bunt infield depth (fast pitch).

Double-play depth (slow pitch).

Double-play depth (fast pitch).

Tight infield—cutoff depth (slow pitch).

*Pitcher moves back off mound after releasing ball.

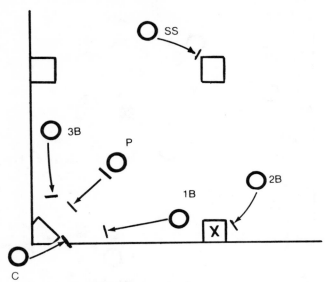

Movement of infielders on bunt
(1st base occupied).

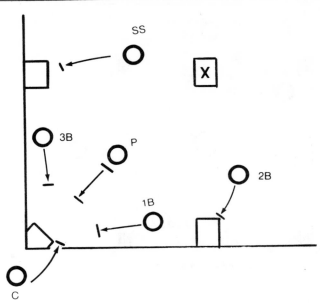

Movement of infielders on bunt
(2nd base occupied only).

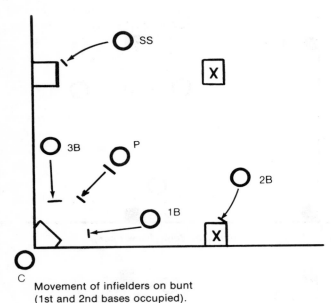

Movement of infielders on bunt
(1st and 2nd bases occupied).

SHORTSTOP—FAST PITCH

A shortstop should have a strong and accurate arm since he or she makes the longest throws of the infielders. Like the second baseman, the shortstop must be alert and be able to anticipate the play.

In most cases, the shortstop plays a little deeper than the second baseman, particularly with no runners on base. However, with a runner on first, the shortstop pulls in slightly and prepares for several situations. If the batter bunts, he or she covers second base for a possible force-out. In the event a left-hander is at bat, the shortstop may have to cover second on the steal. The shortstop also covers second if a grounder is hit to the first or second baseman. In addition, he or she must be ready to field a grounder and make the appropriate play at either first or second base.

Playing the Bunt

When it appears that a sacrifice bunt is coming, the shortstop moves in and toward second base. As soon as the hitter squares off in the bunting stance, the shortstop heads for second, watching the hitter. After the bunt is dropped, he or she covers second. If the bunt is fielded quickly, the play will probably be made at second. In this case, the shortstop takes the throw, tags the bag, and looks for a possible play at first to complete a double play.

If the throw on the bunt play is made at first, the shortstop covers third. This is necessary since the third baseman may have to move near home plate to make the play on the bunt. As a result, the third baseman does not have time to get back to the bag.

When first and second are occupied, the shortstop forgets about second and covers third on the bunt. This is a difficult play, since the shortstop often has to take the throw on the run. Coaches should spend extra time working on this play, since it requires nearly perfect timing.

A shortstop must be particularly alert when only second is occupied. It is his or her job to cover third either on a bunt or an attempted steal. Not only must the shortstop get to the bag quickly, he or she must also tag the runner because no force play is involved. Alert teams often fake a bunt, then have the runner steal in this situation. Consequently, the third baseman must move in for the bunt, and the shortstop must cover third.

Double Play

A major concern in making double plays is to be sure the shortstop is playing close enough to second. Remember, the shortstop must reach second in time to receive the throw, tag the base, and get rid of the ball before the base-runner can break up the play.

When the shortstop receives the ball from the second baseman, it should hit him or her above the waist an instant before reaching the base. The shortstop then steps past the bag with the left foot, drags the right foot across the bag, and throws the ball. If the shortstop takes the throw from the first baseman, the throw should be made to the inside of the bag. The shortstop comes to a quick stop and touches the bag with the left foot, then throws to first.

Outfield Play

On long base hits to left and center field, the shortstop handles the relay throw. As soon as the shortstop determines a base hit is going between the outfielders, he or she heads for short left or short center field.

Just before the outfielder retrieves the ball, the shortstop calls for the throw. When the relay is made at third, the throw is made on the fly, in most cases, since it is a fairly short throw. But when a long throw is required to home, a one-bounce peg is best.

SHORTSTOP—SLOW PITCH

A slow-pitch shortstop must cover considerable ground. Therefore, he or she plays deep, making long throws on many plays. Although the shortstop doesn't have to worry about covering steals and bunts, he or she is involved in many force plays at second and frequent double-play situations.

An outstanding shortstop must be extremely fast, have good reflexes, and should have a strong and accurate arm. When the shortstop in slow pitch has to go between the normal shortstop position and third base, it takes a remarkable play to get the runner at first. First, he or she must make a backhand stop, then make a long hard throw on the line. This is one time the infielder usually throws overhand rather than sidearm. A strong arm is an advantage, but the ability to throw accurately and quickly is equally important. A shortstop with a strong but inaccurate arm is more of a liability than an asset.

THIRD BASE—FAST PITCH

The fast-pitch third baseman must possess extremely quick hands and move like a cat. This player must contend not only with hot line drives, but also handle slow, topped grounders between third and the shortstop.

One of the main jobs of the third baseman is fielding bunts. As a result, he or she plays closer to the hitter than any other infielder. The normal position taken by the third baseman is ten to twelve feet in front of the bag. When an obvious bunt situation exists, the third baseman moves even closer. The moment the hitter indicates a bunt, the third baseman charges forward with feet well spread so he or she can move quickly in any direction.

Once the bunt is down, it is the catcher's responsibility to call out the base. Whenever possible, the play should be made at second. However, if the bunt is well placed, the play will usually be made at first, the second baseman covering the bag. After the throw is made to first, the third baseman hustles back to the bag in case the shortstop fails to cover third and the runner heading for second tries for third.

First and Second Occupied

On a bunt situation with runners on first and second, the third baseman must be extremely cautious. To get the force at third, the bunt must be fielded almost immediately, and the throw must be very accurate to the shortstop covering third. Should the third baseman have any reservations about making this play, it's best to forget the force at third and go for the out at first.

Anytime there is less than two outs with first and second occupied, the third baseman has to be very alert. First, the runners may try a double steal. Because the third baseman plays in front of the bag, he or she has to return quickly to take the throw from the catcher. Also, the team may try a delayed steal, the runners waiting until the catcher starts to throw the ball back to the pitcher and then taking off.

Double Play

With a runner on first, the third baseman fields a grounder and makes the throw to the second baseman. The throw should meet the second baseman an instant before he or she reaches second and should be slightly to the inside of the base.

When first and second are occupied, there are a couple of considerations. After fielding the grounder, the third baseman immediately tags the bag for one out. The throw is then usually made to first, since the runner is ordinarily unable to run from home to first as quickly as the baserunner goes from first to second. Yet, the throw to second is shorter. The speed of the runner on first and the hitter must be considered in each instance. This consideration should be performed prior to the play rather than after the ball is hit. A good infielder always thinks about the next play.

Guard the Line

A hit that gets by the third baseman on his or her right usually results in an extra base hit. So, with nobody on base and particularly with two outs, the third baseman plays back and close to the foul line. A disadvantage of playing back and close to the line is the possibility that the

Special drill for teaching infielders how to use barehand pickup.

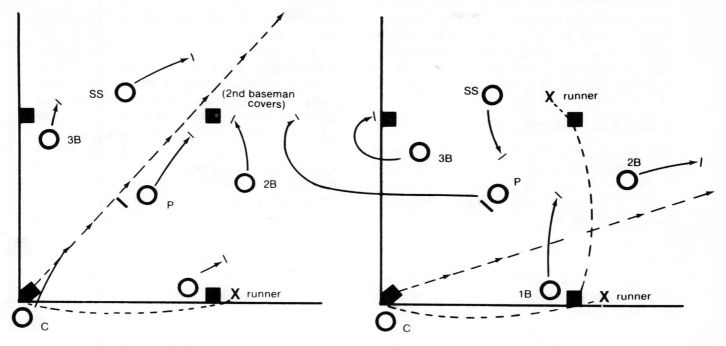

Movement of infielders on single to center field (nobody on).

Movement of infielders on single to right field (runner on first).

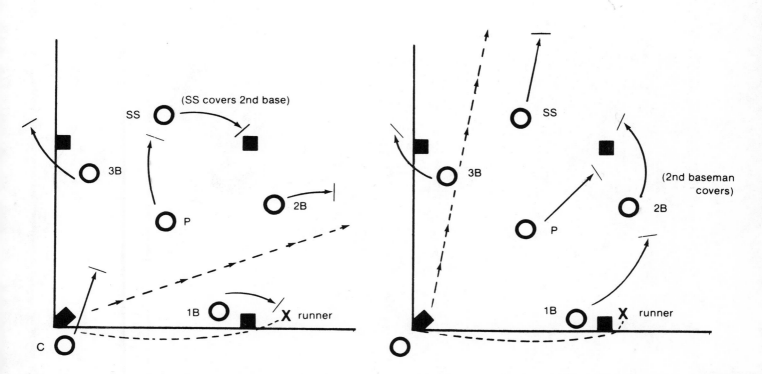

Movement of infielders on hit to right field (nobody on).

Movement of infielders on single to left field (nobody on).

hitter may try a drag bunt. If the hitter does this, the third baseman must charge the ball. Often this play requires a bare-handed pickup and a hurried throw. Coaches should use special drills for this type of play.

THIRD BASE—SLOW PITCH

The slow-pitch third baseman should be an excellent fielder with quick hands but doesn't necessarily have to be speedy. A big, strong, hard-hitting person with average speed and a good arm can play this position well. This player doesn't have to charge bunts or get back to third on steals.

Most third basemen play deep. The normal position is within a few steps behind the bag. Since the slow-pitch third baseman plays deep, many of the throws to first are overhand. Since there are many baserunners in slow pitch, the third baseman is involved in a variety of plays. He or she should be especially adept at making a quick, accurate throw to second. Because a baserunner cannot leave the bag until the pitch reaches the plate, there are many opportunities for force-outs or double plays at second.

7

Outfield Play

FAST PITCH

An outfielder can be no less skillful than any other player. It is a must for an outfielder to be an alert individual, always concentrating on the game. The player who must be in the midst of the action may never become comfortable as a fast-pitch outfielder.

Maintaining total concentration while standing alone in the openness of the outfield takes more self-discipline than being in the tension-charged infield.

Physical ability alone does not make a good outfielder. Without the proper mental makeup a physically talented outfielder can be a big disappointment. Heads-up ball cannot be overemphasized. Good outfielders must know:

A. the rules of the game
B. the special ground rules
C. the score of the game
D. the inning
E. how many are out
F. the hitters
G. the baserunners
H. where the play is going to be on a fly or grounder
I. the outfield terrain
J. the wind patterns of an enclosed or partially enclosed outfield
K. the obstacles and restrictions of the outfield periphery
L. the pitchers

Knowing the hitter and the pitch, for example, may give enough edge to make an impossible play possible. A heads-up outfielder may not even try to catch an easy foul fly when there is a runner on third in the last inning of a tie game with none or only one out.

Outfielders must charge ground balls.

Special Tips

In fast pitch, charging the grounder is essential. If he or she has carefully studied the terrain, the thinking outfielder will make an extra effort to handle grounders before they reach a bare or uneven spot. Bad hops can cause a bobble, even allow the ball to get past the fielder.

The wind can pose problems to an outfielder when judging the fly ball. This is particularly true when there are large obstructions near the playing area. These obstructions often cause eddy currents that raise havoc with otherwise routine fly balls. When the outfielder is unaware of this situation an easy out can become an extra base hit.

If the outfield is not enclosed, outfielders must play a little deeper. This is done to reduce the risk of the ball getting past the fielder. It is fundamental that outfielders back each other up, but in an open outfield it becomes crucial.

Understanding the capabilities and unusual characteristics of the pitcher will help in figuring what to expect. It is good to know if a certain pitcher eases up when the count is against him or her. Perhaps the pitcher is more effective against the pull hitter or has trouble with the left-handed hitter. This information influences

where the outfielder will play the hitter and often determines whether or not the fielder will have a play on the ball.

Knowing the baserunner's habits, speed, and abilities can help in anticipating where the throw should be made.

The outfielder's attention must be on the ball until it is caught and completely under control. Then with a glance the outfielder must evaluate the events taking place on the base paths. However, when the outfielder is confronted with an unexpected situation, he or she must delay the throw until determining where it should be made.

Look for Faults

The coaching staff accepts a substantial amount of responsibility for the performance of outfielders. A player may be making trade offs in his or her mental and physical performance and be unaware of it. It takes careful evaluation to determine whether those diving one-hand

The outfielder's attention must be on the ball until it is caught and under control.

outfield are made by players who feel more confident going either to the right or the left. Drills can overcome these weaknesses and give the player the confidence needed to broaden his or her range of coverage.

It is natural for the outfielder to want to take fly balls in the way he or she has the most confidence. Catching fly balls is considered the most fundamental function of the outfielder, and his or her pride demands that it be done well.

Cover All Aspects

It is up to the coach to see that outfield practice is properly balanced. This means moving in different directions. Flies, line drives, and plenty of grounders should be a part of each practice. The outfielder needs practice to develop and maintain all-around fielding skills.

Most fast-pitch softball games are characterized by few hits and low scores. This makes the extra base more critical than in slow pitch. Allowing a single to become a double may lose the game. Getting throws to the infield quickly and accurately can be a key in the outcome of the game. With the bases only sixty feet apart, the throw to the infield cannot be sloppy.

Prepare for the Throw

Fast-pitch softball is a game of split seconds. Success depends on fundamentals and skills sharpened with practice. These simple rules should be basic to the throw in every case.

A. Know what you are going to do with the ball.

B. Get in the best throwing stance at the time of the catch.

C. Get rid of the ball as quickly as possible without jeopardizing the accuracy of the throw.

D. Never throw behind a runner.

Knowing where to make the throw cannot be overemphasized. It is important to get rid of the ball quickly but not at the expense of a bad throw. If it takes an extra second to get a firm grip on the ball, take it. While you have the ball you have control, but after you have released a bad throw no one has control. Mistakes are greatly reduced if the ball is thrown ahead of

Long fly ball should be caught over shoulder like a football. Never backpedal.

grabs are truly outstanding performances or judgment errors caused by playing too deep. A player who is uncomfortable taking a fly over his or her shoulder may unconsciously play a little too deep. One indication that an outfielder may have this problem is a tendency to backpedal. This should be given prompt attention.

The backpedaler not only contributes to losses but stands a good chance of breaking his or her neck. Similar compromises in playing

Outfield throws are made with overhand motion.

the runner. Never throw behind a runner.

When possible, catching the ball at chest or shoulder height gives good position for making a quick throw. Time can be shaved off the throw by being in motion toward the infield when making the catch. This requires timing and pays off by adding momentum to the throw.

A correct throw by an outfielder is no different than any other skill. This practice must include throws for different situations. Throws to the relay person should be kept above his or her waist to save time for the relay person's throw. Ideally, the throw to the catcher will have a low trajectory, take one bounce, and reach him or her just below the waist. If the catcher is stationed just to the third-base side of the plate, he or she will receive the ball in the best position to make the tag.

Many plays at the plate are close. When a catcher is about to be hit by a charging runner, catching the ball and making the tag can be tough. The one-hop throw is much easier for the catcher to grab and get under control before the collision. Many runs have been scored by jarring the ball loose from a catcher who failed to get a firm hold on the ball.

Throws from the outfield should be made using a three-quarters or overhand delivery. This will keep the throw on a straight course. The infield player receiving the throw usually has enough distractions without trying to follow a long curving peg.

Before the Game

Each outfielder should carefully check out the field prior to the game. This may be done during batting practice, or if no batting practice is permitted it can be done during the infield-outfield drill preceding the game.

Look for bumps or irregularities in the terrain. Often bare spots are created where outfielders stand, and during the course of a season these areas can get quite large. These bare spots can become bumpy, particularly if the field has been played on after a rain. A wise outfielder will try to pick up a grounder in front of these spots.

See if the grass is tall or if it's been freshly mowed. A grounder has to be charged quickly if the grass is tall. However, if the grass is short, the ball is likely to take fast hops or bounce high. Also, expect the grass to become damp when playing night games. Normally the more grass, the damper the field will become.

Check Obstructions

Take a look at the distance you can run for a foul fly. Many fields contain fences close to the foul line. Other fields have light poles placed in playable foul territory. Also, look for bullpen areas that may have pitchers' rubbers or holes that may interfere with the outfielders' attempt to make catches.

Night Light

When playing a night game look at the spots where a high pop fly would normally be hit. In some instances, lights are poorly adjusted and shine directly into the players' vision. The good outfielder will be prepared to shade his or her eyes if lights are poorly placed. Check for lights located in concession stands or in the press box that could obstruct the view on low line drives. If the lights cannot be shaded or turned off, the outfielder must shade his or her eyes.

Sunlight

Nothing can be more troublesome than sun in the afternoon. Then outfielders should wear sunglasses or darken the area under the eyes. Even the finest outfielder in baseball can lose a fly in the sun. Carefully check the location of the sun every inning and practice shading your eyes prior to the first pitch. Batting practice or outfield drills before the game are valuable for learning to properly shade the eyes. In practice it's best if the person hitting fly balls hits from as close to home plate as possible. This permits the outfielders to follow the ball at the same

Before each inning, outfielders should check sun, practice shading eyes.

angle a fly ball would come from an actual hitter.

Wind

The direction and velocity of the wind can be determined if there are flags located in the ball park. If no flags are present, the direction of the wind as well as its velocity can be checked fairly accurately by throwing a few blades of grass in the air. Wind direction and velocity should be checked prior to the game and at the start of each inning. When the wind is blowing toward the hitter, outfielders may play slightly closer than usual. If it's blowing toward center field, the outfielder must obviously play a little deeper than normal. However, when there is a cross wind it is more difficult to determine where to play. Should the wind happen to be blowing hard from left field to right field, the left fielder usually plays slightly more toward center field. The center fielder plays about normal depth but shifts toward right field. A right fielder plays a little deeper than usual, slightly closer to the foul line. When the wind is blowing hard from right field toward left field, the positioning of the outfielders is reversed.

Opposition Lineup

Coaches should go over the lineup with all players, but this is particularly important to outfielders. When the outfielder knows that a certain hitter pulls the ball or swings late, he or she can get positioned quickly. Experienced managers contend that smart outfielders must make spectacular plays only when the hitter hits the ball to a spot different from where he or she normally hits it. Normally the alert outfielder is in the right place. On the other hand, an outfielder who is not alert frequently makes difficult attempts because he or she fails to play the hitter properly.

Outfielder Placement

There are many factors important in deciding where an outfielder should play. In addition to the conditions of the field and wind, the number of outs, the number of baserunners, the hitter, the inning, and the score are factors that must be considered.

As a rule, fast-pitch outfielders play in closer than those in baseball or slow pitch. This placement is not a reflection on the hitters, it's the result of the pitcher dominance in fast pitch. When two outstanding pitchers oppose one another it is not uncommon for each to have ten to twelve strikeouts in a seven-inning game. In

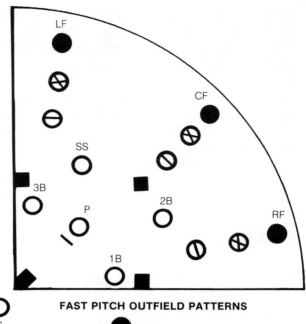

FAST PITCH OUTFIELD PATTERNS

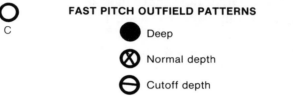

● Deep

⊗ Normal depth

⊖ Cutoff depth

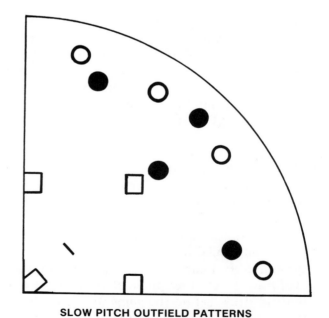

SLOW PITCH OUTFIELD PATTERNS

○ Four deep outfielders

● Three deep outfielders and one short fielder.

these games, the hitters seldom get solid wood on the ball.

Of the few hits made, most are bloopers or short line drives that fall between the outfielders and infielders. So most coaches encourage outfielders to play close, particularly when an outstanding pitcher is on the mound. The exception is when the game is played in a field not enclosed by an outfield fence. Outfielders are forced to play deeper on an open field, otherwise a line drive or hard-hit grounder can go between them for extra bases or even a homer.

During a game, adjustments are made according to the situation. In the case where a runner on third represents the winning run, the coach must examine all alternatives. If the game is in the late innings with none or one out, the outfielder should be brought in. This allows the outfielders to grab low line drives or short pop flies that otherwise may drop in. Sometimes it's possible to throw a runner out at home on a grounder base hit. In the event a long fly is hit, the run will score regardless. So it's best to play percentages. However, if this situation arose early in the game, it would be best to play the outfield at normal depth. Then if the hitter hit a long fly, the run would score but the out would be made.

A hitter's capability plays a big role in deciding where an outfielder plays. With a long-ball hitter up it's only sensible to play deep, particularly if there's no one on base with two outs. On the other hand, let's assume a left-handed punch hitter is at bat. In this instance, it's best to bring the left and center fielders in close and leave the right fielder in the usual position. The rationalization for this move is that the short-ball hitter has less power to the opposite field. But if the hitter hits one on the nose and pulls it, he or she can get fairly good distance.

RIGHT FIELDER

One of the most essential parts of the right fielder's job in fast pitch, backing up throws at first, is often neglected by coaches. In addition to normal plays made at first, pick-off throws and pegs on bunts are difficult plays to make, and the possibility of an overthrow is high.

A good coach will work on backup maneuvers for right field. As soon as the hitter squares to bunt, the right fielder should begin his or her move toward the foul line in case the throw goes astray.

Because the right fielder must make the longest throw to third, a strong arm is beneficial. However, it is not absolutely essential, since there are not that many plays at third in fast pitch. Being able to get rid of the ball quickly and throw accurately is more important.

The right fielder should back up the center fielder whenever possible. On a seemingly easy high pop fly to center, encourage the right fielder to back up center field. There are many things that can happen. A ball may be lost in the sun, the center fielder could slip, or he or she could lose it in the lights. When the right fielder hustles to back up, the runner can be kept from getting an extra base in case something happens. In fact, the right fielder may even catch the ball if he or she is in good position.

Right Field Hits

A right fielder should charge all ground balls. The fielder scoops up the ball and prepares to throw in one smooth motion. If the hit is a single with none on, he or she quickly throws the ball to second. Some fielders make the mistake of pausing to look at the hitter rounding first. A good baserunner often tries to draw the throw at first by rounding the base, tempting the fielder to throw behind him or her. Rarely will the outfielder catch a runner this way. Disregard this play and always throw directly to second.

If first base is occupied and the hit is a sharp single to right, the right fielder makes the throw to third. Since this requires a long throw, encourage the fielder to throw low with a one-bounce peg. This throw is much easier to handle.

A hit to right with a runner on second usually scores the runner. It is rare that a throw will nail the runner at home. Therefore, the fielder should disregard the runner going home and throw to second. This fundamental is one of the most difficult things for a coach to teach. Even in the major leagues an experienced outfielder will sometimes try to throw the runner out at home. In most instances, the outfielder fails to get the runner at home, and the hitter goes to second on the throw. When a young player

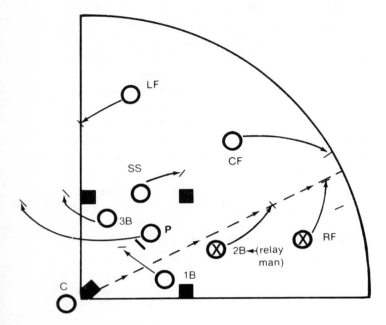

Movement of fielders for relay throw or extra base hit to right field. Right fielder throws to second baseman. Center fielder backs up right fielder.

persistently tries to throw the runner out at home, the coach must clearly explain that unless the fielder has been pulled in close to cut the men off at the plate, it's important to throw to second. Remember, it's easier to score from second than from first. In addition, when the player holds the runner on first there is the possibility for a force-out, even a double play.

When a hit gets past the right fielder and goes deep toward the fence, the second baseman normally becomes the relay person. The throw to the relay person should be made quickly and accurately. There is no advantage to a relay unless the throw is easily handled by the second baseman. Often, teaching the outfielder to properly use the relay is neglected. It is one of the most important fundamentals for the outfielder to get down.

One of the best ways to teach a player how to complete a relay is to break the lesson into several steps.

1. Get to the ball quickly.
2. Learn to anticipate bounces off the fence.
3. After reaching the ball grab it firmly.
4. Pivot and look for the relay person.
5. Make the throw overhand, not sidearm.
6. Aim for the waist or chest of the relay.

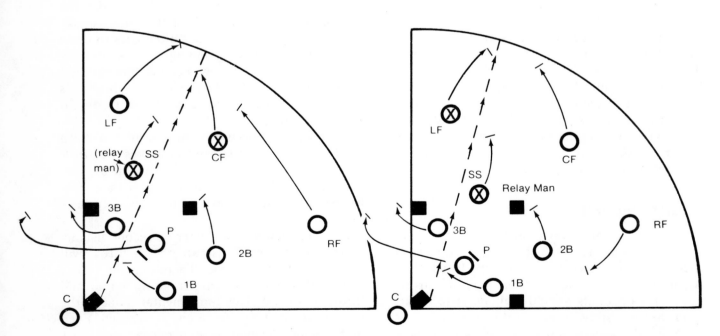

Movement of fielders for relay throw on extra base hit to left center field. Center fielder throws to shortstop.

Movement of fielders for relay throw on extra base hit to left field. Left fielder throws to shortstop.

CENTER FIELDER

In fast pitch, the center fielder must be one of the most versatile players on the team. This position should be handled by someone who is fast, has quick reactions, and fields both grounders and flies equally well. Most coaches play the center fielder a little more shallow than the right and left fielders. This positioning permits the center fielder to cover low, hard line drives that otherwise might become singles. In addition, it gives them a chance at short pop fly balls. Although natural speed is an advantage for the center fielder, the ability to get a jump on the ball is even more important. A player with good reactions and excellent fielding skills will make an outstanding center fielder. A strong arm is also an advantage but not necessary.

The center fielder has more responsibilities than the other two outfielders. Consequently, he or she must be a fine student of the game. Besides backing up both the right and left fielders, the center fielder must be alert for overthrows at second. Infielders can get confused and be late in covering second on a steal attempt. The better teams in fast pitch prepare their outfielders for backing up throws on steals and force plays. For example, when a steal is likely, the infielders not only signal the catcher who will cover the bag, but also the center fielder. As a result, the center fielder is better prepared to back up the throw in case it gets away from the infielders.

Hit to Center Field

Since the center fielder normally plays closer, his or her throws to second or even third are often made on the fly. Of all the players, the center fielder has a better perspective of where the ball is going once it comes off the bat. This gives the center fielder an opportunity to get an excellent jump on the ball. As a result, the center fielder has the best opportunity of throwing out a runner going from second to home. When to try to get the runner at home in this situation is learned best through experience. However, the center fielder must consider several things: how hard the ball is hit, the speed of the runner, and the importance of the potential run.

Hard hit balls that get past the center fielder usually require a relay play. Tips for the right fielder on handling relay throws are applicable to the center fielder. However, which infielder he or she hits on the throw depends on where the ball goes. For example, on a deep hit to right center field, the second baseman usually takes the throw. But when the hit is toward deep left center, the shortstop is most likely to handle the relay.

LEFT FIELDER

Backing up the third baseman is a prime responsibility of the left fielder. In fast pitch, the shortstop often covers third on a steal or sacrifice bunt. This is one of the most difficult plays to execute, since the shortstop takes the throw from the catcher or infielder while on the move. Consequently, the chance for an overthrow is greater than on a normal infield play.

With a man on second, the left fielder must always be prepared to back up third. As soon as the batter squares to bunt or the runner breaks for third, the left fielder must move toward the foul line. Once the bunt is down, he or she quickly covers for the possible overthrow. If the bunt goes to the pitcher or first baseman, the left fielder will have to run into foul territory to get the proper angle. But if the bunt goes along the third base line, the fielder should be closer to the foul line to cover.

For all practical purposes, the left fielder does not need a strong arm, since he or she does not make long throws to third. Nevertheless, the left fielder usually makes more plays than the right fielder, since most hitters are right-handed. Therefore, the left fielder most handle grounders well and be capable of covering a lot of ground.

Hit to Left

Fast-pitch left fielders are often confronted with handling punch hits by left-handed batters. Because of the pitching speed of most pitchers, many fast-running left-handed hitters punch at the ball rather than take a full cut. Low line drives coming off the bats of these left-handed hitters often curve and are difficult to handle. With this type of hitter at bat, the left fielder ordinarily plays shallower than usual. On a single, the left fielder must charge the ball to prevent a double. Also, he or she must not let tricky hops get through. In some cases, it's best to block the ball with the knee or body, particularly when the outfield is rough.

In most cases, the left fielder throws the ball on the fly to second on a single. There are two primary reasons for this. First, the fielder is usually making a relatively short throw. Second, throwing a one-bounce peg is a little risky. Since there is often a ridge of turf at the junction of the grass and infield, a ball can take a bad hop when it hits this area. When it's necessary to make a bounce peg to second, the left fielder should aim the throw a few feet outside the infield.

The shortstop is the person to take the relay on hits that get past the left fielder. Because the left fielder is usually throwing to home or third on extra base hits, he or she sometimes completes the throw without the relay. Whether the left fielder hits the relay person depends on the size of the field, his or her arm, and where the ball is retrieved. Often the shortstop or center fielder help the left fielder by shouting instructions as to where the left fielder should make the throw. This is particularly important when the fielder is chasing the ball and has his or her back to the infield.

OUTFIELD—SLOW PITCH

Fundamentals for slow-pitch outfielders are similar to those of fast pitch. Fielding, throwing, and backing up are virtually the same. However, slow-pitch outfielders need not worry about backing up infielders on bunts or steals.

The physical requirements and skills of the slow-pitch outfielder are slightly different than those of fast pitch. First, the slow-pitch outfielder must play deeper than in fast pitch. There are many more long balls hit in slow pitch. As a result, the outfielder must be able to come in fast as well as have a strong arm.

In slow pitch, the outfielder has to make the same plays required in fast pitch, but more often. Since the pitcher is dominant in fast

pitch, the outfielder does not have to contend with a number of plays during an average game. However, in slow pitch the outfield can expect to make many plays in nearly every game.

There are two popular ways of positioning the outfielders in slow pitch. Some coaches prefer to use four outfielders, deep and fairly evenly spaced. The reason for playing four deep outfielders is to reduce the number of hits that would normally go through a three-man outfield. Other coaches prefer to use three deep outfielders, the fourth, the shortfielder, shallow. Fast-pitch rules formerly called for ten players, and the shortfielder was a key position.

Playing four deep gives a team the advantage of decreasing the number of extra base hits. But this pattern has the disadvantage of allowing short pop flies and low line drives to fall in for base hits. A major reason for using a shortfielder is to reduce the number of hits just behind the infield. In addition, the shortfielder may be used as another infielder. Of course, the disadvantage of this pattern is the open spaces created between the three deep outfielders. Because slow-pitch hitters have become adept at placing the ball as well as hitting long line drives, the four-deep pattern seems to be the most popular way of playing the outfield.

Some coaches prefer to use a combination of the shortfielder and the four deep players, depending on the situation. For example, if a slow runner is on first, one of the outfielders is placed directly behind second. As a result, it's hard for the hitter to get a grounder through the infield, and the possibility for a double play is much greater. The shortfielder also improves the chances of cutting down the winning run with a runner on third.

Defensively, the slow-pitch outfielder is much more important than in fast pitch. A fast-pitch team which has an outstanding pitching staff can often sacrifice defense for hitting, at least at one position. This is not true in slow pitch. The slow-pitch outfielder must field extremely well, have a strong arm, and be fast. If he or she happens to be an excellent hitter also, that is an additional bonus.

8

Hitting and Running Bases

HITTING

There are three basic reasons why the inexperienced player often has difficulty hitting fast-pitch deliveries. First, the hitter doesn't realize how fast the ball is moving. Second, the hitter isn't taking the rise or drop of the ball into account. Third, the hitter is swinging too hard.

All three can be helped by good coaching. Many believe good hitters are born, not made. While it is certain that size, eyesight, and reflexes play an important role, many experienced coaches and players believe that concentration and a desire to do well play an even bigger part.

Fast Pitch

What is little known about fast-pitch softball is that a top fast-pitch pitcher can throw a softball as fast as a baseball pitcher can throw a

baseball. But because the softball pitcher stands only forty-six feet from the plate, it only takes about .4 second for the ball to get to the plate compared to about .7 second for the baseball.

While the softball is larger, it doesn't necessarily make a better target. It drops, rises, and curves more than a baseball, because it has a larger surface area to "grip" the air.

Because of this, it's often difficult for even a good baseball player to hit well right away in softball. This has led some people to believe that playing softball will ruin a young player's chances for a career in baseball. But that just isn't true. The player's timing and judgment simply need time to adjust.

Young players are often told to keep their swings level. While it is important for the young player to develop a smoothly grooved swing, the swing has to be adjusted to the pitch. To hit a drop ball, the swing has to be much like hitting a golf ball. To hit a high rise, the swing has to come down on the ball. The level swing is used only when the pitch is about down the middle and belt high.

Most young players like the idea of hitting with power. Often they believe that the way to do this is to swing a long, heavy bat as hard as they can. But unless the player is unusually big or strong, a long, heavy bat just doesn't come around fast enough to connect.

The young player should select a bat that is the right length and weight for him or her. Often the correct bat is quite a bit shorter and lighter than the player would have picked. Even when the right bat is found, it might be necessary for the player to choke up on the handle for better control. Some of the best softball hitters take the full grip for the first two strikes, then choke up to gain better control when the count is against them.

The On-Deck Circle

The time a player spends in the dugout and the on-deck circle is often wasted. This time should be spent studying the pitcher. The player should watch every move the pitcher makes to see if there is anything he does to tip the pitches. The on-deck batter should swing the bat in time with the pitcher's delivery to get the feel of the pitcher's rhythm.

When the batter gets in the batter's box, softball (and baseball) pretty much boils down to a one-on-one situation. The batter must put everything except that competition out of his or her mind, study the pitcher at every opportunity.

At the Plate

Whether the pitcher likes to throw quickly or slowly and deliberately, once the batter gets into the box he or she should immediately get ready. Some batters have a habit of swinging the bat as they wait for the pitch. All that swinging does little but waste time and often results in the batter not being ready for the pitch.

Stance

The word *stance* has often been taken to mean both the position of the batter's feet in the box, and the position of his or her whole body.

Referring to the position of the feet, the batter's stance is described as open, square, or closed. In an open stance, the front foot is placed farther away from the plate than the rear foot. This stance is often used by pull hitters. In the square stance, the most common, both feet

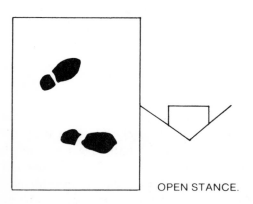

OPEN STANCE.

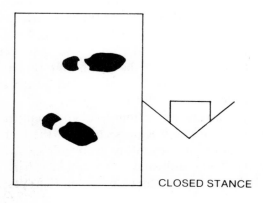

CLOSED STANCE

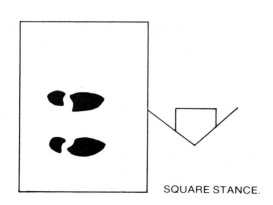

SQUARE STANCE.

Batter's body is nearly erect as he or she gets set for pitch.

probably not try to change it. If the player is having trouble, and no other changes or extra practice help, perhaps modifications should be tried.

It is likely that in the past too much emphasis has been placed on the importance of the batter's stance.

Stride

A smooth stride and swing should be the goal of every player. Some experts believe that consistent hitting can only be achieved after the stride and swing are polished.

In fast pitch, it is important that the stride be coordinated with the pitcher's delivery. Striding too early or too late will throw off the swing.

The stride should be relatively short, about six to eight inches, and should be made by sliding the forward foot straight ahead slightly above ground. Young players occasionally get into the habit of stepping away from the plate when striding. This habit can be hard to break later.

Often an overanxious batter will hurry the stride. This usually results in swinging ahead of

are the same distance from the plate. They are spaced twelve to eighteen inches and point directly at the plate.

In a closed stance, the front foot is placed closer to the plate. An opposite-field hitter will typically use this stance.

The batter's body as he or she gets set for the pitch should be nearly erect. The weight should be evenly distributed on the balls of the feet, knees slightly bent. As long as it doesn't adversely affect the swing, the angle at which the player holds the bat is unimportant.

The batter's hips and shoulders should be level, arms bent at the elbows and held away from the body. It is important that the batter keep the elbow of the rear arm shoulder high. With the elbow high, he or she can get up on the rise ball more consistently. If the rear elbow starts to drop, the batter will have difficulty meeting the rise ball.

Most often, the player will automatically take the body and foot stance most comfortable to him or her. Unless the player's stance is clearly causing hitting problems, the coach should

Stride should be about six to eight inches.

Near point of contact, weight is transferred to front foot and rear leg begins to bend.

As swing is completed, wrists roll over on follow-through.

Greatest power is realized immediately at point of contact.

the ball. If the batter tries to adjust his or her timing to compensate for a hurried swing, he or she may miss the ball.

A hitter who strides too early can delay this by twisting the front hip toward the plate just before striding. This delay will not affect the proper position of the batter's arms.

The Swing

As the pitcher delivers the ball, the batter begins to stride and swing. At the beginning of the swing, the batter has his or her wrists cocked. As the swing is continued, the batter's arms straighten at the elbow, but the wrists remain cocked. Dropping the wrists reduces the chance of hitting the ball solidly. At contact, the batter's weight is transferred to the front foot, and the rear leg begins to bend. At this point, the swing has its most power. As the swing is completed, the wrists roll over and the follow-through is completed.

At contact, the batter's front leg should be straight, the back leg bent at the knee. The

coach should check a batter who consistently shows a long stride and bent front leg.

"Hit It Where It's Pitched"

The technique for hitting an inside pitch at a different point than an outside pitch is called "hitting the ball where it's pitched."

If the ball is inside, the batter should hit it in front of the plate. If the pitch is outside, hit it at the back of the plate. A right-handed player will hit an inside pitch to the left, the left-handed hitter to the right.

When the ball is pitched across the heart of the plate, right- and left-handed hitters meet it smack in the center of the plate.

A player weak on inside pitches should not move away from the plate but should take extra practice in meeting the ball in front of the plate. Moving away from the plate will just make it that much harder to hit outside pitches. In the same way, a player weak on outside pitches usually weakly hits the ball on the end of the bat or misses it altogether.

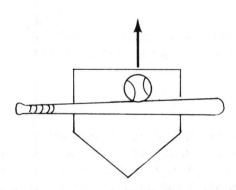

Figure A. Ball pitched over heart of plate is hit into middle of the diamond.

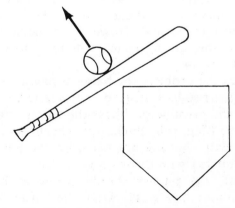

Figure B. It's best to meet the inside pitch in front of the plate.

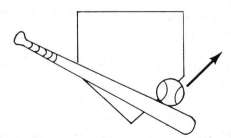

Figure C. Hitters should not try to pull outside pitch. Outside pitch is met at rear of plate.

Getting More Hits

While improving a batting average is important, there are generally two situations when getting more hits becomes a real concern—the inexperienced player and the experienced player in a slump.

An inexperienced player may get the finest instruction on grip, stance, stride, and swing, but if he or she doesn't practice hard, the instruction will be of minimal help.

Along with practice, the inexperienced player needs to face progressively tougher competition. A player improves most when competing with someone better than himself or herself.

For a player to develop a good batting average, he or she must face good pitchers. If the player faces only average pitchers, he or she will be helpless when first facing a really outstanding one. If this should occur, the coach should be careful not to have the player make any drastic changes in style. Instead, the coach should encourage the player by saying that as he or she faces better pitchers, he or she will start meeting the ball more often.

Once in a while, even an excellent batter may get into a slump. When this happens, often only encouragement and patience are needed to get things back to normal. However, if the slump continues, the batting coach will have to find out what is wrong.

Perhaps the problem the batter is having is in meeting the rise ball. Instead of trying to determine all the possible problems the batter might have in hitting this pitch, the coach should schedule extra batting practice with the player facing a pitcher who throws a good rise.

At first, the pitcher should throw at half speed without any stuff. After the batter has had a few minutes to loosen up, the pitcher should begin to throw at three-quarter speed with some rise on the ball. The coach should have the batter swing above the pitch. After a few swings above the pitch, the batter can go to a normal swing. When the batter starts hitting the three-quarter-speed rise consistently, the pitcher should begin throwing an occasional full-speed rise. This kind of practice should be repeated for at least several days. If the batter has trouble hitting the drop ball, he or she should practice swinging under the ball at first.

A good batting coach can often correct a batter's fault after watching him or her swing for only a few minutes. A player having trouble should get advice from the coach, not from other players. And he or she shouldn't attempt to solve the problem alone.

The Batting Tee

One of the innovations that has helped inexperienced or slumping batters is the "batting tee." The batting tee is a piece of nonrigid, but not floppy, plastic pipe about two inches in diameter that has been set about two feet into the ground much like a fence post. The top of the pipe is between belt and shoulder height.

To practice with the tee, the batter puts a ball onto the end of the pipe, much like a golfer would tee up a golf ball. Then the batter swings at the ball as though it were a pitch frozen in midair.

The object is for the batter to practice "grooving" his or her swing to drive the ball cleanly off the tee. Although the tee doesn't provide the drop or rise pitch, a smoothly grooved swing can make facing a pitcher with good stuff a lot easier.

If part of the field is available, setting several tees at different heights can provide practice in grooving the swing for a variety of "pitch" combinations.

Bunting

As in baseball, there are two different kinds of bunts used in fast pitch: the sacrifice and the drag bunt. (The squeeze bunt, in which a runner on third starts for home as the ball is pitched and the batter attempts to bunt the ball to allow the runner to score, is really a variety of either the sacrifice or the drag.) A properly executed bunt can be as effective as an extra base hit.

The Sacrifice Bunt

As the name implies, the sacrifice bunt means that the batter is sacrificing his or her chances for a base hit by clearly showing the other team that he or she is going to bunt.

The batter's goal in the sacrifice is to allow a

Sacrifice bunt hitter slides top hand near trademark. Bat rests loosely on fingertips with thumb gripping top of bat.

baserunner to move forward. Because the play is a sacrifice, the batter must make sure he or she gets the bunt down properly rather than trying to get out of the box too quickly.

A sacrifice bunter should stand near the front of the box. This gives him or her a better chance to put the ball down fair. As the pitcher begins delivery, the batter usually brings the rear foot in line with the front one, feet about twelve to eighteen inches apart. If the batter feels more comfortable nearer the plate, he or she can drop the front foot back to be in line with the rear one.

When taking the bunting position, the hitter slides the top hand along the bat to a spot near the trademark without moving the bottom hand. In the full position, the batter faces the pitcher, hands well spread on the bat, knees and hips slightly bent, weight on the balls of the feet.

While there is no specific way to hold the bat with the top hand, most experienced bunters let the bat rest loosely on the fingertips with the thumb gripping the top of the bat. Held this way, the bat will move back into the web between the thumb and index finger when the ball hits it. This acts as a shock absorber, especially on a fast pitch, and allows a lot of the speed to be dissipated. The batter does not swing, but positions the bat and holds it still, parallel to the ground.

The batter must hit the ball on the lower part of the bat, so it is hit onto the ground. If the ball hits the upper part of the bat, it will be popped up. This kind of pop-up can cause a double play.

The opposing pitcher will try to cross up the bunter, often by throwing a rise ball.

Because the first and third basemen play close

On drag bunt, hitter starts normal stride. Just before ball reaches plate, hitter slides top hand up six to eight inches.

on sacrifices, the batter should direct the ball toward the pitcher. Directing the ball isn't easy in fast pitch, but it can be done.

To place the ball toward the pitcher, the bunter places the bat straight across the plate. To bunt toward third, the right-handed batter places the bat as though he or she were trying to pull a hit down the third base line. To bunt toward first, the batter angles the bat toward right field.

The Drag Bunt

The drag bunt is intended to get the hitter on base. Its key is surprise. The batter gives no indication of a bunt until the last moment.

The batter begins to take a normal swing, but just before the ball reaches the plate he or she slides the top hand six to eight inches up the handle.

Since the batter takes a normal stride, his or her weight is on the front foot when contacting the ball. As contact is made, the batter con-

tinues to stride toward first. The bunter hits and runs at the same time. The element of surprise coupled with the fast break for first can make it work.

If the first attempt to drag bunt results in a foul or a miss, the batter can swing on the next pitch. This may force the first and third basemen to play in, a short fly going over their heads for a base hit.

The left-handed bunter has the advantage of being a step or so closer to first than the right-handed batter.

RUNNING BASES

Hitting the ball squarely is only half the job, getting every base possible is the other half. A batter who pauses at the plate has probably thrown away an extra base hit. The sacrifice bunt is an exception.

The batter has to be set to break for first the instant that the bat makes contact.

When the batter hits the ball into the outfield,

On final move of drag bunt, batter is bunting and running at the same time.

he or she should run two feet or so outside the foul line. Approaching first, he or she times the stride for a sharp turn, catching the inside corner of the bag with the right foot.

If the ball goes into center or right field, the batter can generally tell if it's a single or an extra base hit. If the ball is hit into left field, though, the batter should look to the first-base coach. Otherwise the batter may lose the stride rhythm.

If the hit is clearly a single, the batter rounds the bag a step or two, quickly making a judgment. If the fielder has possession, the runner stays at first. However, the runner must not turn his or her back on the play, because the fielder might make an error.

If the hit appears to be for extra bases, the batter will have to decide whether or not to head for third. If the hit is to left field, the runner can usually decide what to do. On a hit to right field, where the runner can't see without

slowing up, he or she will probably have to look to the third-base coach for advice.

On an advance to third as a result of an extra base hit, another batter's hit, or an attempted steal, the runner must look to the third-base coach for guidance.

On an advance to the plate, a runner might look to the on-deck batter for advice, if the play doesn't develop too quickly.

Stealing

Once the runner is safe, the next goal is to advance. And one of the most exciting ways to advance is the steal. Regardless of how fast the runner is, he or she isn't likely to steal many bases if he or she waits until the pitch is well on its way toward the plate. Since the rules don't allow the runner to leave base until the ball leaves the pitcher's hand, the runner has to anticipate the release. The break from base must

Start of straight-in slide. Top leg is nearly straight, bottom leg bent. Practice slides in stocking feet to prevent injuries.

At completion of straight-in slide, bottom leg will be drawn up to rise quickly.

be made the instant the pitcher releases the ball.

Sliding

Taking every possible base occasionally results in the runner and a throw getting to a base at about the same time. When that happens, the slide is helpful. The runner will have a better chance of avoiding the tag and will stand less chance of injury.

There are three types of slides: the straight-in, the hook or fall-away, and the headfirst. The first two are feet first. And while the headfirst is spectacular, it should be avoided by inexperienced players.

The hook or fall-away is generally used when the runner knows from which direction the throw will come.

When the fielder takes the throw on the inside, the runner hooks to the outside. The runner hurls his body to the right in this case away from the fielder, and hooks the bag with the left toe or instep. If the throw is outside, the slide is reversed.

When the runner can't tell where the fielder will take the throw, the straight-in slide, the headfirst slide for the daring, is probably best. The straight-in slide is made by keeping the top leg nearly straight and bending the bottom leg at the knee. The advantage of the straight-in slide is that the runner draws up the bottom leg when making contact with the base. In this position the runner rises quickly and can perhaps take another base in the event of a bobble.

A slide started too late usually will not be effective and can result in injury to the runner or fielder. It's embarrassing for a runner to slide

Start of hook slide.

Completion of hook slide.

too early and come to a stop a foot short of the bag.

HITTING AND RUNNING THE BASES— SLOW PITCH

The fundamentals of base running discussed under fast pitching apply equally to slow pitch. Hitting in slow pitch, though, requires some different techniques.

First, a batter used to fast pitch will almost certainly find his or her timing off. The batter will probably also take his or her eyes off the ball and swing too hard. In slow pitch, the ball crosses the plate in a downward arc. If the pitch is shoulder high, the batter will have to swing down. If the pitch is knee high, the batter will have to swing up.

The player who times the pitch, develops a smooth swing, and learns to place hits can enjoy many years of slow-pitch softball with a good batting average.

9

Umpiring

FAST PITCH

Because the two-person umpiring system is standard for most leagues, our comments are limited to this technique. Excellent instructions for three-person systems, as well as general umpiring techniques, can be found in the *Softball Umpire's Manual,** from which this chapter has been abstracted.

The plate umpire, in addition to calling balls and strikes, must also take a share of base plays. When more than one runner is on, the leading runner becomes this umpire's responsibility as soon as the fate of a batted ball is determined. To do this, this umpire goes into the infield, then watches the lead runner.

The base umpire is responsible for seeing that

_____
*Amateur Softball Association of America, Oklahoma City, Oklahoma.

runners touch first and second and calls whatever play may be made on the batter once he or she becomes a baserunner. Once the batter advances beyond second, however, that batter becomes the plate umpire's responsibility. The base umpire must make his or her decision quickly and announce it loudly. This will enable the plate umpire to judge whether a runner attempting a score has reached home before the tag.

The position for the base umpire is about ten feet in foul territory along the right field foul line, a step farther from the plate than the first baseman. Being this far to the rear, the umpire is out of the way of any move the first baseman may make for a drive down the foul line. From this position it is easy to dash into the infield to call plays at first.

On a ball hit to the third baseman the umpire should rush to a position a few feet toward the pitcher's side of an imaginary line running from first to second base. On a throw from the short-stop the umpire should move to an imaginary line between first and second, outside the dia-mond.

Many good umpires stand immediately back of first base in foul territory, but this position is not recommended. Their view of the play may be as good, but they are at a disadvantage in covering second on an overthrow.

Study Rule 10 in the *Official Softball Guide & Rulebook*. This details the umpire's duties, important for you to know.

SITUATION: NO RUNNERS ON BASE

Plate Umpire:

1. Call all hit balls fair or foul. Move in front of plate to see the ball. Don't call foul balls too soon. Hustle.

Key:

P-Plate Umpire
B-Base Umpire
R-Runner or Runners

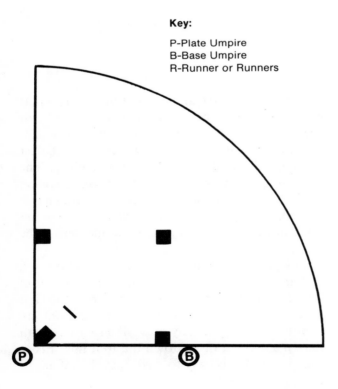

Situation: No runners on base. (fast pitch)

2. On infield ground hits close to the foul line, stay at home and make the call, then move toward third for a possible play. Stay in foul territory.
3. In addition to being in position to make a call at third, be ready to help your partner in case of a rundown. If the play is close, move in on it and make your call with emphasis.

Base Umpire:

1. Base umpire takes position one to fifteen feet beyond first in foul territory.
2. On balls hit to the left side of the diamond, move into the infield about fifteen feet, slightly outside the path between first and second.
3. On balls hit to the right side of the diamond, move up to the line, staying in foul territory between the base line and the coaches' box. Be careful to stay out of the way of the batter-runner.
4. On clean hits, move into the infield and carry the runner all the way to third.
5. On sharply hit balls to right field, move out quickly to determine whether the ball has been trapped. Make your call quickly and emphatically. This is particularly important in night games.
6. Hustle. Be in the correct position on all calls.

SITUATION: RUNNER ON FIRST

Plate Umpire:

1. Call all hit balls fair or foul. Move in front of the plate to better see the ball. Don't call foul balls too soon. Hustle.
2. On infield ground hits close to the foul line, stay at home and make the call, then move toward third for a possible play. Stay in foul territory.
3. In addition to being in position to make a call at third, be ready to help your partner in case of a rundown. If the play is close, move in on top of it and make your call with emphasis.
4. On hits, take the lead runner into third and home. On steals where the throw to second is wild, pick up the runner coming into third.

5. If the initial play of a batted ball is made on the baserunner, watch the batter touch first and be prepared to help your partner.

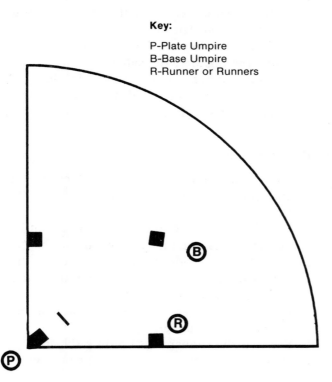

Situation: Runner on first. (fast pitch)

Base Umpire:

1. Take a position about halfway between first and second, outside the base line. This will normally place you two or three steps behind and to the right-field side of the second baseman.
2. If the runner attempts to steal second, move toward the base. If the throw is wild, move inside base paths and be prepared to pick up the runner going to home. Plate umpire covers third.
3. On flies to outfield, move into infield to a position between pitching rubber and base line.
4. See that runner and batter touch first and second.
5. On a double-play attempt, follow the ball and move toward the closest play. Let the ball turn you on all throws.
6. Hustle and be in the correct position.

SITUATION: RUNNER ON SECOND ONLY

Plate Umpire:

1. Call all hit balls fair or foul. Move in front of plate to better see the ball. Don't call foul balls too soon. Hustle.
2. On infield ground hits close to the foul line, stay at home and make the call, then move toward third for a possible play. Stay in foul territory.
3. In addition to being positioned to make a call at third, be ready to help your partner in case of a rundown. If the play is close, move on top of it and call with emphasis.
4. On hits, take the lead runner into third and home.
5. If the initial play of a batted ball is made on the baserunner, watch the batter touch first and be prepared to help your partner with the call.
6. On hits, move toward third. If the lead runner comes home and there is no play made there, watch the runner touch home.

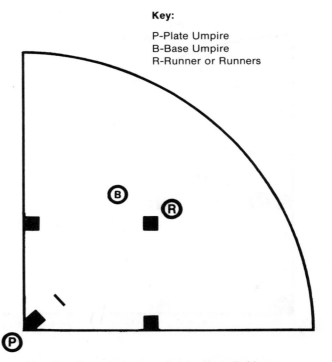

Situation: Runner on second only. (fast pitch)

Base Umpire:

1. Take a position two or three steps behind and to the center-field side of the shortstop.
2. On any ball hit to the infield, cover the first throw by moving toward that base and inside the infield. If first throw is to first or second, plate umpire is to cover any subsequent throw to third.
3. On flies to the outfield, move to infield between pitching rubber and base path, lining up on the lead runner. See that he or she tags up after catch.
4. On wide open plays at first and fly balls hit to the outfield, stay at second and be alert for snap throws.
5. On hits to the outfield watch the runner touch each base and take that runner into third.
6. On attempted steal of third, move toward third.
7. Hustle. Be in the correct position.

Key:

P–Plate Umpire
B–Base Umpire
R–Runner or Runners

Situation: Runner on third only. (fast pitch)

SITUATION: RUNNER ON THIRD ONLY

Plate Umpire:

1. Call all hit balls fair or foul. Move in front of plate to better see the ball. Don't call foul balls too soon. Hustle.
2. If a fly is hit, line up the runner on third and watch the tag after the catch.
3. On hits, move toward third. If the lead runner comes home and there is no play made there, watch the runner touch home.

Base Umpire:

1. Take a position two or three steps behind and slightly to the center-field side of the shortstop.
2. If a ball is hit to the infield, wait until a fielder moves, then move toward that base.
3. Call all plays made on the first throw of the ball. Take the runner into third and see that all bases are touched.
4. Be alert for snap throws and pick-off attempts on the runner.
5. See that the runner tags up on a fly.
6. Hustle. Be ready to back up your partner.

SITUATION: RUNNERS ON FIRST AND SECOND

Plate Umpire:

1. Call all hit balls fair or foul. Move in front of plate to better see the ball. Don't call foul balls too soon. Hustle.
2. On infield grounders close to the foul line, stay at home and make the call, then move toward third for a possible play. Stay in foul territory.
3. In addition to being in position to make a call at third, be ready to help your partner in case of a rundown. If the play is close, move in and make your call with emphasis.
4. On hits, take the lead runner into third and home.
5. With less than two outs, be on the alert for the infield fly rule.
6. If the initial play is made on the baserunner, watch the batter touch first and be prepared to help your partner.

Key:

P-Plate Umpire
B-Base Umpire
R-Runner or Runners

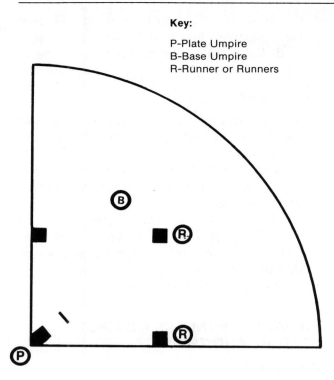

Situation: Runners on first and second. (fast pitch)

SITUATION: RUNNERS ON SECOND AND THIRD

Plate Umpire:

1. Call all hit balls fair or foul. Move in front of plate to better see the ball. Don't call foul balls too soon. Hustle.
2. If a fly is hit, line up the runner on third and watch the tag-up after the catch.
3. On hits, move toward third, but watch the first runner touch home and the second runner touch third, then take that runner to the plate.
4. On hits to the infield where the throw is to third, take the first runner to the plate and watch the batter touch first. If the play is to first, watch the first runner touch the plate and move to third for a possible play on the second runner.

Base Umpire:

1. Take a position between the shortstop and second, about two or three steps behind the shortstop.

7. On hits, move toward third. If the lead runner comes home and there is no play made there, watch the runner touch home.

Base Umpire:

1. Take a position between the shortstop and second, a few steps behind the infielders.
2. Be alert for the infield fly rule with less than two out and call it concurrently with your partner.
3. On a hit, watch the runner from first touch second, then pick up the batter. If the plate umpire stays at home for a possible play, make all calls at either base.
4. On a ball hit to the infield, call the initial play at any base.
5. On fly balls to the outfield, watch the runners tag up. Move into the infield to be in position to see any plays.
6. Hustle. Be in the correct position.

Key:

P-Plate Umpire
B-Base Umpire
R-Runner or Runners

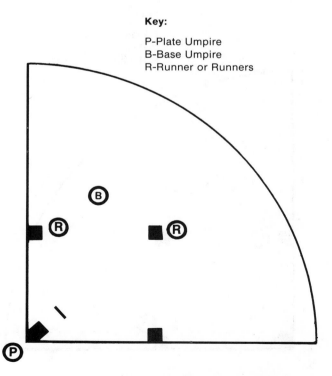

Situation: Runners on second and third. (fast pitch)

2. Take all plays at any base made on the initial throw of the ball.
3. On flies, line up the runner on second while the plate umpire lines up on the runner at third. See that the runner tags up at the catch and take that runner into third.
4. Take the batter-runner into third.
5. Hustle. Watch for snap throws and pick-off attempts.

SITUATION: RUNNERS ON FIRST AND THIRD.

Plate Umpire:

1. Call all hit balls fair or foul. Move in front of plate to better see the ball. Don't call foul balls too soon. Hustle.
2. On infield ground hits close to the foul line, stay at home and make the call, then move toward third for a possible play. Stay in foul territory.
3. If a fly is hit, line up the runner on third and watch the tag-up after the catch.

Key:

P—Plate Umpire
B—Base Umpire
R—Runner or Runners

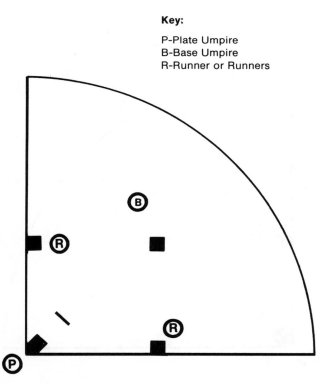

Situation: Runners on first and third.

4. On hits, move toward third. If the lead runner comes home and there is no play made there, watch the runner touch home.

Base Umpire:

1. Take a position between the shortstop and second, about two or three steps behind the shortstop.
2. Take the initial throw of a batted ball, except to the plate. If a play is close, move in on it. Watch for snap throws.
3. On a hit, watch the runner from first touch second and be alert for a play at that base. Take the runner as far as third and watch that runner touch each base.
4. Hustle. Be in the correct position.

SITUATION: RUNNERS ON FIRST, SECOND, AND THIRD.

Plate Umpire:

1. Call all hit balls fair or foul. Move in front of plate to better see the ball. Don't call fouls too soon. Hustle.
2. Line up the lead runner and see that he or she does not leave the base too soon on fly balls. If no play is made there, move toward third and watch the runner touch the plate.
3. On a hit to the infield along the base line with the runner coming in from third, line up the play from behind the plate.
4. On other hits to the infield, move toward third and watch the lead runner touch the plate if the throw is made toward second or first. If the throw is to third or second, watch the runner touch first and the runner from third touch home.

Base Umpire:

1. Position yourself between shortstop and second, two or three steps behind the shortstop.
2. On balls hit to the infield, take the play on any throw except to the plate. If the throw is to the plate, be alert for a snap throw to any base.
3. On hits to the outfield, move inside the infield and be prepared to make calls at first, second, or third.

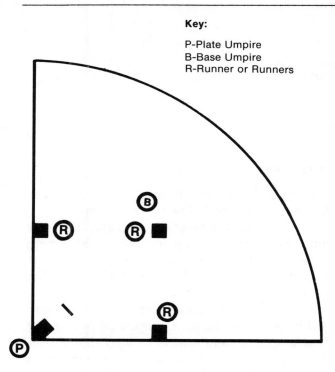

Key:

P-Plate Umpire
B-Base Umpire
R-Runner or Runners

Situation: Runners on first, second, and third. (fast pitch)

Base Umpire:

Assume a position along the foul line approximately fifteen feet from first toward home. Stand near the line in foul territory and face the infield. Hustle players on and off the field. Brush the pitching rubber after the pitcher has taken his or her warm-up pitches.

Both Umpires:

Each umpire should stand in an erect position, relaxed. Do not stand with your arms folded. Hustle. Be proud. Be professional.

SLOW PITCH

Plate Umpire:

The plate umpire has the same responsibilities as in fast pitch. In slow pitch, the plate umpire is responsible for all calls at third and home. This is to include even the first throw of a batted ball if the play is at third or home.

This system is designed to allow the plate umpire more active participation. It is simple mechanics and will be easy to work if you hustle.

4. On hits, watch the runner from first touch second, then pick up the runner and stay with that runner all the way. Be alert for the runner from first to second, then go back in. Be alert for a rundown and snap throws.
5. Line up runners two and three on flies and be alert for infield flies with less than two outs.
6. Watch the runners touch each base.
7. Hustle. Never take your eyes off the ball.

BETWEEN INNING MECHANICS

Plate Umpire:

Assume a position along the foul line approximately fifteen feet from home. Stand near the line in foul territory and face the infield. Alternate your position from left to right field foul lines so you are always on the side of the field that the team coming off the field crosses to enter their bench area. This is also the best time to obtain additional spare game balls.

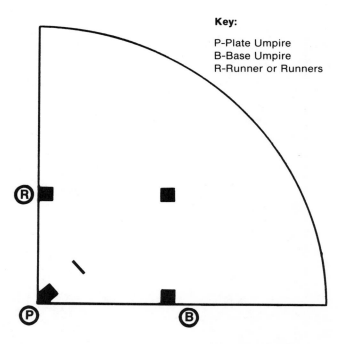

Key:

P-Plate Umpire
B-Base Umpire
R-Runner or Runners

Situation: No runners on, or runner on third only. (slow pitch)

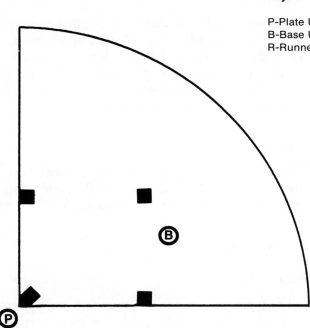

Key:

P-Plate Umpire
B-Base Umpire
R-Runner or Runners

Situation: All situations other than those described in Fig. 8. (slow pitch)

Base Umpire:

Responsibilities are basically the same as in fast pitch with the following exceptions:

1. Anytime a runner is on base, the base umpire will take a position two or three steps behind and to the right of the second baseman. The base umpire will never take a position between second and third.

2. Under normal conditions, all calls at third will be made by the plate umpire. However, the base umpire should always be alert. Should the plate umpire have to stay at home and there is a snap throw to third for another play, the base umpire would have to make the call.

10

Offensive Strategy

If a coach had nine great hitters, there would be little need for offensive strategy. To field a top-notch team, the good coach must sacrifice hitting for defense at several positions. Fast pitch in particular is geared to a strong defense. Most coaches place great emphasis on developing a near flawless infield combination. As a result, it is impossible to field nine outstanding hitters.

Although an outstanding infielder may not be a natural hitter, he or she must be well coordinated. Any person with good physical coordination can be taught some of the finer points of offense—bunting, stealing, hitting behind the runner. A well-placed bunt, just moving the runners will win games.

During practice, it is important to point out that bunting is different from hitting. Hitting requires an active, coordinated movement of several body parts. Bunting is a passive function.

When hitting a ball, the shoulders, arms, wrists, hips, and legs are moving at contact. When bunting, the body is frozen at contact. The bat should merely steer the ball.

How far and where the ball goes on a bunt depends on three factors: angle of the bat, angle of the ball and bat contact, and how firmly the bat is held. If the ball hits the center of the bat, this will result in a line drive toward first. However, should the ball hit the bottom of the bat, this will result in a soft grounder toward third.

When the bat is held loosely, the ball contact is cushioned and the offense gets a jump. The best bunt comes off the bat softly, moving toward the pitcher. A bunt is one of the most powerful offense tools but only when properly executed.

ANALYZE SITUATION

Although the sacrifice is a great offensive weapon, it is not always the best play with a runner on first and nobody out. Several things should be considered. Is the hitter a good bunter? Is the runner on first fast? Is the batter or batters who follow the bunter good percentage hitters? If the answer to any one of these is no, the sacrifice will not increase the probability of scoring.

When a coach decides to use the sacrifice, he or she concedes 33-1/3 percent of his offensive opportunity just to advance the runner. For example, a good fast-pitch infield will often throw the runner out at second. In this case, the offense loses one out. Furthermore, an attempted sacrifice may be popped up and turned into a double play.

Many coaches who prefer the sacrifice with a runner on first and no outs claim there is an excellent chance that the defense will make an error. Although this may be true with an average defense, a good fast-pitch infield plays the bunt as well as a grounder.

With a runner on first and nobody out, there are other opportunities to advance the runner. You can leave the runner on first. An infield play at first, single, or an extra base hit will still advance the runner.

One alternative is to substitute a speedster at first. This provides the option of stealing or using the drag bunt. Furthermore, a speedy runner will usually go to third on an outfield single, even score.

A sacrifice with runners on first and second and no outs is a better percentage play than when only first base is occupied. One of the best situations for the sacrifice exists when only second base is occupied. The runner can get a good jump, and it is difficult to put the runner out at third. With no outs and third occupied, a squeeze play is also an excellent move. In this situation, the play at home must be a tag.

FAKE BUNT AND STEAL

The fake bunt and steal works well when second, or first and second, is occupied. On the fake, the third and first basemen charge, leaving third uncovered for the steal. The only way to defense this move is for the shortstop to cover third, and the play must be a tag. Timing is the key. The fake must come at the last moment.

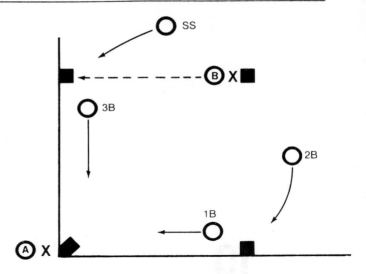

Fake bunt and steal: Hitter (A) fakes bunt, runner (B) steals third. Shortstop must try to cover third on this play.

STEAL AND BUNT

Fast-pitch teams rarely use the steal and bunt, although it can turn a game around. Probably the best time to use this play is with a runner on first, one or two outs, and a right-hander at bat. If the second baseman normally covers the steal on this play, it should work well. The play begins when the runner breaks for second on a steal, then the hitter drop bunts. If the bunt is well executed, the runner on first will beat the throw to second and first will be uncovered. Runners are now on first and second without the loss of an out.

HIT AND RUN

With a right-hander at the plate, the runner on first breaks for a steal. As the second baseman covers second, the batter pokes the ball through the area vacated by the second baseman. Even if the second baseman recovers in time to field the ball, it is unlikely he or she will get the runner at second, let alone the hitter. When executed correctly, the hit and run usually advances the runner on first to third. A speedster can sometimes score. The hit and run is not often used in fast pitch, nevertheless, when it works, it is an excellent move.

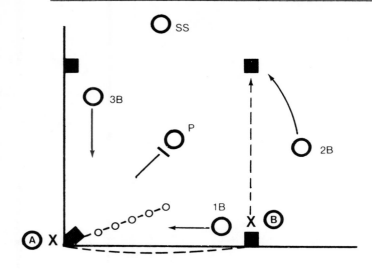

Steal and bunt: Runner (B) steals with right-handed hitter at bat. Second baseman moves to cover second. Hitter (A) bunts toward pitcher or first. First is left uncovered. Play can be used with men on first and second.

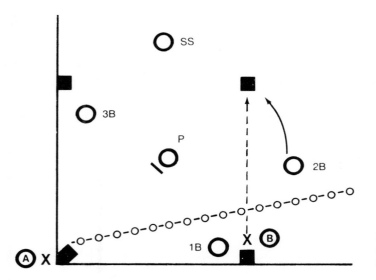

Hit and run: Runner (B) steals. Second baseman moves to cover second. Hitter (A) hits ball through hole left by second baseman.

SIGNALS

No play will be successful unless all players and coaches involved perfectly execute their portion of the offensive maneuver. A great share of this responsibility lies with the coach's ability to communicate the signal clearly. The rest of the job depends on the players' ability to read the sign and then perform.

When either the hitter or the runner misses the sign or misinterprets it, the play usually fails. This mistake turns a potential advantage into a significant disadvantage. It could mean the difference between winning and losing.

Signals must be designed so they are not easily picked up by the opponents. However, they cannot be so complicated that they persistently confuse the hitters and runners. A good coach will use a key sign followed by the specific sign that indicates what play is to be used.

11

Official Softball Rules

RULE 1. DEFINITIONS

Sec. 1. Altered Bat. A bat is considered altered when the physical structure of a legal bat has been changed. Examples of altering a bat are replacing the handle of a metal bat with a wood handle or other type handle, inserting material inside the bat or adding foreign substance, such as paint to a bat. Replacing the grip with another legal grip is not considered altering the bat.

Sec. 2. Appeal Play. An appeal play is a play upon which an umpire cannot make a decision until requested by a player or coach. The appeal must be made before the next pitch, legal or illegal.

Sec. 3. Base on Balls. A base on balls permits a batter to gain first base without liability to be put out and is awarded to a batter by the umpire when 4 pitches are judged to be balls.

Sec. 4. Base Path. A base path is an imaginary line 3 feet (0.99 m) to either side of a direct line between the bases.

Sec. 5. Baserunner. A baserunner is a player of the team at bat who has finished his turn at bat, reached first base, and has not yet been put out.

Sec. 6. Batted Ball. A batted ball is any ball that hits the bat or is hit by the bat and which lands either in fair or foul territory. No intention to hit the ball is necessary.

Sec. 7. Batter's Box. The batter's box is the area to which the batter is restricted while in position with the intention of helping his team to obtain runs. The lines are considered inside the batter's box.

Sec. 8. Batter-Baserunner. A batter-baserunner is a player who has finished his turn at bat but has not yet been put out or touched first base.

Sec. 9. Batting Order. The batting order is the official listing of offensive players in the order in which members of that team must come to bat. When the line-up card is submitted it shall also include the players' position.

Sec. 10. Blocked Ball. A blocked ball is a batted or thrown ball that is touched, stopped, or handled by a person not engaged in the game, or which touches any object which is not part of the official equipment or official playing area.

Sec. 11. Bunt. A bunt is a legally tapped ball not swung at, but intentionally met with the bat and tapped slowly within the infield.

Sec. 12. Catch. A catch is a legally caught ball which occurs when the fielder catches a batted or thrown ball with his hands or glove. If the ball is merely held in the fielder's arms or prevented from dropping to the ground by some part of the fielder's body or clothing, the catch is not completed until the ball is in the grasp of the fielder's hands or glove. It is not a catch if a fielder, immediately after he contacts the ball, collides with another player or wall or falls to the ground, and drops the ball as a result of the collision or falling to the ground. In establishing a valid catch, the fielder shall hold the ball long enough to prove he has complete control of the ball and that his release of the ball is voluntary and intentional. If a player drops the ball while in the act of throwing it, it is a valid catch.

Sec. 13. Catcher's Box. The catcher's box is that area within which the catcher must stand while and until the pitched ball is batted or reaches home plate. The lines are to be considered within the catcher's box.

Sec. 14. Charged Conference. A charged conference takes place when:
a. The defensive team requests a suspension of play for any reason, and . . .
b. A representative (not in the field) of the defensive team enters the playing field and gives the umpire cause to believe that he has delivered a message (by any means) to the pitcher.

Sec. 15. Chopped Ball (SP Only). A chopped hit ball is one at which the batter strikes downward with a chopping motion of the bat.

Sec. 16. Coach. A coach is a member of the team at bat who takes his place within the coach's lines on the field to direct the players of his team in running the bases. 2 coaches allowed.

Sec. 17. Dead Ball. The ball is not in play and is not considered in play again until the pitcher has the ball in his possession and is within 8 feet. (2.64 m) of the pitcher's plate and the plate umpire has called "play ball."

Sec. 18. Defensive Team. The defensive team is the team in the field.

Sec. 19. Dislodged Base. A dislodged base is a base dislodged from its proper position.

Sec. 20. Double Play. A double play is a play by the defense in which two offensive players are legally put out as a result of continuous action.

Sec. 21. Fair Ball. A fair ball is a batted ball that settles on fair territory between home and first base or home and third base; or that is on or over fair territory including any part of first and third base when bounding to the outfield; or that touches first, second, or third base; or that, while on or over fair territory, touches the person of any umpire or player; or first falls on fair ground beyond 1st and 3rd; or that while over fair territory passes out of the playing field beyond the outfield fence.

Note: A fair fly shall be judged according to the relative position of the ball and the foul line, including the foul pole, and not as to whether the fielder is on fair or foul territory at the time he touches the ball. It does not matter whether the ball first touches fair or foul territory as long as it does not touch anything foreign to the natural ground in foul territory and complies with all other aspects of a fair ball.

Sec. 22. Fair Territory. Fair territory is that part of the playing field within and including the first and third base foul lines from home base to the bottom of the extreme playing field fence and perpendicularly upwards.

Sec. 23. Fielder. A fielder is any player of the team in the field.

Sec. 24. Fly Ball. A fly ball is any ball batted into the air.

Sec. 25. Force-out. A force-out is an out which can be made only when a baserunner loses the right to the base which he is occupying because the batter becomes a baserunner, and before the batter or a succeeding baserunner has been put out.

Sec. 26. Foul Ball. A foul ball is a batted ball that settles on foul territory between home and first base, or between home and third base; or that bounds past first or third base on or over foul territory; or that first falls on foul territory beyond first or third base; or that, while on or over foul territory, touches the person of an umpire or player, or any object foreign to the natural ground.

Note: A foul fly shall be judged according to the relative position of the ball and the foul line, including the foul pole, and not as to whether the fielder is on foul or fair territory at the time he touches the ball.

Sec. 27. Foul Tip. A foul tip is a batted ball which goes directly from the bat, not higher than the batter's head, to the catcher's hands and is legally caught by the catcher.

Note: It is not a foul tip unless caught and any foul tip that is caught, is a strike. In Fast Pitch the ball is in play. In Slow Pitch the ball is dead. It is not a catch if it is a rebound unless the ball first touched the catcher's hand or glove.

Sec. 28. Home Team. The home team is the team on whose grounds the game is played, or if the game is played on neutral ground, the home team shall be designated by mutual agreement or by a flip of a coin.

Sec. 29. Illegal Bat. An illegal bat is one that does not meet the requirements of Rule 3, Sec. 1.

Sec. 30. Illegally Batted Ball. An illegally batted ball occurs when a batter hits a ball while his entire foot is completely out of the box, on the ground when he hits the ball; when any part of the batter's foot is touching home plate when he hits the ball; or when the batter hits the ball with an illegal bat.

Sec. 31. Illegally Caught Ball. An illegally caught ball occurs when a fielder catches a batted or thrown ball with his cap, mask, glove, or any part of his uniform while it is detached from its proper place.

Sec. 32. In Flight. In flight describes any batted, thrown, or pitched ball which has not yet touched the ground or some object other than a fielder.

Sec. 33. In Jeopardy. In jeopardy is a term indicating that the ball is in play and an offensive player may be put out.

Sec. 34. Infield. The infield is that portion of the field in fair territory which includes areas normally covered by infielders.

Sec. 35. Infield Fly. An Infield fly is a fair fly ball (not including a line drive nor an attempted bunt) which can be caught by an infielder with ordinary effort, when first and second, or first, second, and third bases are occupied, before two are out. The pitcher, catcher, and any outfielder who positions himself in the infield on the play shall be considered infielders for the purpose of this rule.

Note: When it seems apparent that a batted ball will be an Infield Fly, the umpire shall immediately declare "Infield Fly" for the benefit of the runners. If the ball is near the baselines, the umpire shall declare "Infield Fly, If Fair."

The ball is alive and runners may advance at the risk of the ball being caught, or retouch and advance after the ball is touched, the same as on any fly ball. If the hit becomes a foul ball, it is treated the same as any foul.

If a declared Infield Fly is allowed to fall untouched to the ground, and bounces foul before passing first or third base, it is a foul ball. If a declared Infield Fly falls untouched to the ground outside the baseline, and bounces fair before passing first or third base, it is an Infield Fly.

Sec. 36. Inning. An inning is that portion of a game within which the teams alternate on offense and defense and in which there are 3 outs for each team.

Sec. 37. Interference. Interference is the act of a defensive player which hinders or prevents a batter from striking or hitting a pitched ball, or the act of an offensive player, which impedes, hinders, or confuses a defensive player while attempting to execute a play.

Sec. 38. Legal Touch. A legal touch occurs when a runner or batter-baserunner who is not touching a base is touched by the ball while it is securely held in the fielder's hand. The ball is not considered as having been securely held if it is juggled or dropped by the fielder after having touched the runner unless the runner deliberately knocks the ball from the hand of the fielder. It is sufficient for the runner to be touched with the hand or glove in which the ball is held.

Sec. 39. Legally Caught Ball. A legally caught ball occurs when a fielder catches a batted or thrown ball provided it is not caught in the fielder's hat, cap, mask, protector, pocket, or other part of his uniform. It must be caught and firmly held with hand or hands.

Sec. 40. Line Drive. A line drive is an aerial ball that is batted sharply and directly into the playing field.

Sec. 41. Obstruction. Obstruction is the act of a fielder, while not in possession of the ball or in the act of fielding a batted ball, which impedes the progress of the baserunner who is legally running bases.

Sec. 42. Offensive Team. The offensive team is the team at bat.

Sec. 43. Outfield. The outfield is that portion of the field which is outside the diamond formed by the baselines or the area not normally covered by an infielder and within the foul lines beyond first and third bases, and boundaries of the grounds.

Sec. 44. Overslide. An overslide is the act of an offensive player when as a baserunner he overslides a base he is attempting to reach. It is usually caused when his momentum causes him to lose contact with the base which then causes him to be in jeopardy. The batter-runner may overslide first base without being in jeopardy if he immediately returns to that base.

Sec. 45. Overthrow. An overthrow is a play in which a ball is thrown from one fielder to another to retire a runner who has not reached or is off base and which goes into foul territory beyond boundary lines of playing field.

Sec. 46. Passed Ball (FP Only). A passed ball is a legally delivered ball that should have been held or controlled by the catcher with ordinary effort.

Sec. 47. Pivot Foot. The pivot foot is that foot which the pitcher must keep in constant contact with the pitcher's plate, until the ball is released.

Sec. 48. "Play Ball." Play ball is the term used by the plate umpire to indicate that play shall begin or be resumed.

Sec. 49. Quick Return Pitch. A quick return pitch is one made by the pitcher with the obvious attempt to catch the batter off balance. This would be before the batter takes his desired position in the batter's box or while he is still off balance as a result of the previous pitch.

Sec. 50. Sacrifice Fly. A sacrifice fly is scored when, with less than 2 outs, the batter scores a runner with a fly ball which is caught.

Sec. 51. Stealing. Stealing is the act of a baserunner attempting to advance during a pitch to the batter.

Sec. 52. Strike Zone.
a. (Fast Pitch) The strike zone is that space over any part of home plate which is between the batter's arm pits and the top of his knees when the batter assumes his natural batting stance.
b. (Slow Pitch) The strike zone is that space over any part of home plate which is between the batter's highest shoulder and his knees when the batter assumes his natural batting stance.

Sec. 53. Time. Time is the term used by the umpire to order the suspension of play.

Sec. 54. Triple Play. A triple play is a continuous action play by the defense in which three offensive players are put out.

Sec. 55. Turn at Bat. A turn at bat begins when a player first enters the batter's box and continues until he is put out or becomes a baserunner.

Sec. 56. Wild Pitch (FP only). A wild pitch is a legally delivered ball so high, so low, or so wide of the plate that the catcher cannot or does not stop and control it with ordinary effort.

RULE 2. THE PLAYING FIELD
(Refer to Drawing Showing Official Dimensions of Softball Diamond)

Sec. 1. The Playing Field Is the Area within Which the Ball May Be Legally Played and Fielded. The playing field shall have a clear and unobstructed area within a radius of 225 feet (74.25 m) (Male and Female Fast Pitch); 250 feet (82.5 m) (Female Slow Pitch); and 275 feet (90.75 m) (Male Slow Pitch) from home plate between the foul lines. Outside the foul lines and between home plate and the backstop there shall be an unobstructed area of not less than 25 feet (8.25 m) in width.

Note: The pitcher's plate shall have a 16 foot (5.28 m) circle drawn from the pitcher's plate, 8 feet (2.64 m) in radius.

Sec. 2. Ground or Special Rules Establishing the Limits of the Playing Field May Be Agreed Upon by Leagues or Opposing Teams Whenever Backstops, Fences, Stands, Vehicles, Spectators, or Other Obstructions Are within the Prescribed Area. Any obstruction on fair ground less than 225 feet (74.25 m) (Male and Female Fast Pitch); 250 feet (82.5 m) (Female Slow Pitch); and 275 feet (90.75 m) (Male Slow Pitch) from home plate should be clearly marked for the umpire's information.

Sec. 3. The Official Diamond shall have 60 foot (19.8 m) baselines with pitching distances as follows: Fast Pitch: Male—46 feet (15.18 m), Female—40 feet (13.2 m); Slow Pitch: Male—46 feet (15.18 m), Female—46 feet (15.18 m).

Sec. 4. The Layout of the Diamond Is Shown in the Accompanying Diagram. To determine the position of home plate draw a line in the direction it is desired to lay the diamond. Drive a stake at the corner of the home plate nearest the catcher. Fasten a cord to this stake and tie knots, or otherwise mark the cord at 46 feet (15.18 m), 60 feet (19.8 m), 84 feet 10¼ inches (27.72 m-256.75 mm), and at 120 feet (39.6 m).

Place the cord (without stretching) along the direction line and at the 46 foot (15.18 m) marker place a stake—this will be the front line at the middle of the pitcher's plate. Along the same line drive a stake at the 84 foot 10¼ inches (27.72 m-256.75 mm) mark—this will be the center of second base.

Place the 120 foot (39.6 m) marker at the center of second base and, taking hold of the cord at the 60 foot (19.8 m) marker, walk to the right of the direction line until the cord is taut and drive a stake at the 60 foot (19.8 m) marker, walk across the field and in like manner mark the outside corner of third base. Home plate, first, and third bases are wholly inside the diamond. To check the diamond, place the home plate end of the cord at first base stake and the 120 foot (39.6 m) marker at third base. The 60 foot (19.8 m) marker should now check at home plate and second base.

Check all distances with a steel tape whenever possible.

The Three-Foot (0.99 m) Line is drawn parallel to and 3 feet (0.99 m) from the base line starting at a point halfway between home plate and first base.

The Batter's On Deck Circle is a 5 foot (1.65 m) circle (2½ foot [0.825 m] radius) placed adjacent to the end of player's bench or dugout area closest to home plate.

The Batter's Box, one on each side of home plate, shall measure 3 feet (0.99 m) by 7 feet (2.31 m). The inside lines of the batter's box shall be 6 inches (150 mm) from home plate. The front line of the box shall be 4 feet (1.32 m) in front of a line drawn through the center of home plate. The lines are considered part of the batter's box.

The Catcher's Box shall be 10 feet (3.3 m) in length from the rear outside corners of the batter's boxes and shall be 8 feet 5 inches (2.64 m-125 mm) wide.

The Coach's Box Is Behind a Line 15 Feet (4.95 m) Long Drawn Outside the Diamond. The line is parallel to and 8 feet (2.64 m) from the first and third baseline extended from the bases toward home plate.

RULE 3. EQUIPMENT

Sec. 1. The Official Bat Shall Be Round, Made of One Piece of Hard Wood, or Formed from a Block of Wood Consisting of Two or More Pieces of Wood Bonded Together with an Adhesive in Such a Way That the Grain Direction of All Pieces Is Essentially Parallel to the Length of the Bat. Plastic and bamboo are acceptable materials for construction of bats. Any such laminated bat shall contain only wood or adhesive, except for a clear finish. The bat shall be no more than 34 inches (850 mm) long and not more than 2¼ inches (56.25 mm) in diameter at its largest part. A tolerance of 1/32 inches (1.3 mm) is permitted to allow for expansion. The bat, in its entirety, shall not exceed 38 ounces (1064 g) in weight. The bat shall have a safety grip of cork, tape, or composition material. The safety grip shall not be less than 10 inches (250 mm) long and shall not extend more than 15 inches (375 mm) from the small end of the bat. The bat shall be marked "OFFICIAL SOFTBALL" by the manufacturer.

The bat may be made of metal. The bat shall have no exposed rivets, pins, rough or sharp edges, or any form of exterior fastener that would present a hazard. All exposed surfaces of the bat shall be smooth and free of burrs. A metal bat shall not have a wooden handle. It shall conform to all of the above specifications with the exception that it is metal instead of wood, plastic, or bamboo. Unless the bat is made of one piece construction with the barrel end closed there shall be a rubber or vinyl plastic insert firmly secured at the large end of the bat.

Sec. 2. The Official Softball shall be a regular, smooth-seam concealed stitch or flat surfaced ball, not less than 11⅞ inches (296.88 mm) or more than 12⅛ inches (303.13 mm) in circumference, and shall weigh not less than 6¼ ounces (175 g) nor more than 7 ounces (196 g). The center of the ball may be made of either No. 1 Quality long fibre Kapok or a mixture of cork and rubber, hand or machine wound, with a fine quality twisted yarn and covered with latex or rubber cement or it may be made of other materials approved by The International Joint Rules Committee on Softball. The cover of the ball shall be the finest quality No. 1 chrome tanned horse or cow hide, cemented to the ball by application of cement to the underside of the cover and sewed with waxed thread of cotton or linen. The cover of the ball may also be made of synthetic material.

Sec. 3. The Home Plate Shall Be Made of Rubber or Other Suitable Material. It shall be a 5 sided figure 17 inches (425 mm) wide across the edge facing the pitcher. The sides shall be parallel to the inside lines of the batter's box and shall be 8½ inches (212.5 mm) long. The sides of the point facing the catcher shall be 12 inches (300 mm) long.

Sec. 4. The Pitchers Plate shall be of wood or rubber, 24 inches (600 mm) long and 6 inches (155 mm) wide. The top of the plate shall be level with the ground. The front line of the plate shall be the following distance from the outside corner of home plate: Male Fast Pitch [46 feet (15.18 m)]; Male Slow Pitch [46 feet (15.18 m)]; Female Slow Pitch [46 feet (15.18 m)]; Female Fast Pitch [40 feet (13.2 m)].

Sec. 5. The Bases, Other than Home Plate Shall Be 15 Inches (375 mm) Square and Shall Be Made of Canvas or Other Suitable Material and Not More than 5 Inches (125 mm) in Thickness. The bases should be securely fastened in position.

Sec. 6. Gloves May Be Worn by Any Player, but Mitts May Be Used Only by the Catcher and First Baseman. No top lacing, webbing, or other device between the thumb and body of the glove or mitt worn by a first baseman or other fielder shall be more than 4 inches (100 mm) in length. The pitcher's glove shall be of one color other than white or grey. Multicolor gloves are acceptable for all other players. Gloves with white or grey circles on the outside, giving the appearance of a ball, are illegal for all players.

Sec. 7. A Shoe Shall Be Considered Official If It Is Made with Either Canvas or Leather Uppers or Similar Materials. The soles may be either smooth or with soft or hard rubber cleats. Ordinary metal sole and heel plates may be used if the spikes on the plate do not extend more than ¾ inches (18.75 mm) from the sole or heel of the shoe. Shoes with rounded metal spikes are illegal.

Sec. 8. Masks must be worn by catchers in Fast Pitch and are recommended in Slow Pitch. Female catchers MUST wear a body protector in Fast Pitch. It is recommended that female catchers wear a body protector in Slow Pitch.

Sec. 9. No Equipment Shall Be Left Lying on the Field, Either in Fair or Foul Territory.

Sec. 10. Uniform. All players on a team shall wear unforms identical in color, trim, and style. Ball caps are considered part of the uniform and are required for male players. Any part of any undershirt exposed to view shall be of a uniform solid color for all players of a team and if worn by more than 1 player, they shall be identical in color. No player shall wear ragged, frayed, or slit sleeves on exposed undershirts or uniform shirt. Male catchers must wear caps. Helmets are permissable for catchers, batters, and baserunners. For safety and injury prevention, exposed jewelry, such as: Wrist Watches, Bracelets, and Neck Chains MUST not be worn during the game.

RULE 4. PLAYERS AND SUBSTITUTES

Sec. 1. A Team Shall Consist of 9 (Fast Pitch) and 10 (Slow Pitch) Players Whose Positions Shall Be Designated as Follows: Pitcher, Catcher, First Baseman, Second Baseman, Third Baseman, Shortstop, Left Fielder, Center Fielder, and Right Fielder. In (Slow Pitch), the 10th player shall be designated as a "Short Fielder." Players of the team in the field may be stationed anywhere on fair ground. The pitcher, in delivering the ball to the batter, must be in legal pitching position and the catcher must be in his box.

Sec. 2. A Team Must Have 9 (Fast Pitch) or 10 (Slow Pitch) Players to Start or to Continue a Game.

Sec. 3. A Player Shall Be Officially in the Game when His Name Has Been Entered on the Official Score Sheet or Has Been Announced. A substitute may take the place of a player whose name is in his team's batting order. The following regulations govern the substitution of players:

a. The captain of the team making the substitution should immediately notify the umpire who will suspend play and announce the change to the scorekeepers.
b. Substitute players will be considered in the game without penalty as follows:
    (1) If a batter, when he takes his place in the batter's box.
    (2) If a fielder, when he takes the place of the fielder substituted for.
    (3) If a runner, when the substitute replaces him on the base he is holding.
    (4) If a pitcher, when he takes his place on the pitcher's plate.
c. Each pitcher whose name has been entered on the score sheet, who has been announced, or who has taken his place on the pitcher's plate, must pitch until the first batter facing him has completed his turn at bat or the side has been retired. Any other

player may be removed from the game at any time.
d. Whether announced or unannounced, any play made by or on the substitute player shall be legal.
e. A player removed from the game shall not participate in the game again except as a coach.
    EFFECT—Sec. 3e: The game shall be forfeited to the offended team.
f. No player shall take a position in the batter's line of vision or with deliberate unsportsmanship intent, act in a manner to distract the batter.
    EFFECT—Sec. 3f: The offender shall be removed from the game and an illegal pitch shall be declared, even though a pitch may not be released.

RULE 5. THE GAME

Sec. 1. The Choice of the First or Last Bat in the Inning Shall Be Decided by a Toss of a Coin Unless Otherwise Stated in the Rules of the Organization under Which the Schedule of Games Is Being Played.

Sec. 2. The Fitness of the Ground for a Game Shall Be Decided Solely by the Plate Umpire.

Sec. 3. A Regulation Game Shall Consist of Seven Innings.

a. A full seven innings need not be played if the team second at bat scores more runs in six innings or before the third out in the last half of the seventh inning.
b. A game that is tied at the end of seven innings shall be continued by playing additional innings, or until one side has scored more runs than the other at the end of a complete inning, or until the team second at bat has scored more runs in their half of the inning before the third out is made.
c. A game called by the umpire shall be regulation if five or more complete innings have been played or if the team second at bat has scored more runs than the other team has scored in five or more innings. The umpire is empowered to call a game at any time because of darkness, rain, fire, panic, or

other cause which puts the patrons or players in peril.

d. A regulation tie game shall be declared if the score is equal when the game is called at the end of five or more completed innings, or if the team second at bat has equaled the score of the first team at bat in the incomplete inning.

e. These provisions do not apply to any acts on the part of players or spectactors which might call for forfeiture of the game. The umpire may forfeit the game if attacked physically by any team member or spectator.

f. A forfeited game shall be declared by the umpire in favor of the team not at fault in the following cases:

(1) If a team fails to appear on the field or, being on the field, refuses to begin a game for which it is scheduled or assigned at the time scheduled or within a time set for forfeitures by the organization in which the team is playing.

(2) If, after the game has begun, one side refuses to continue to play, unless the game has been suspended or terminated by the umpire.

(3) If, after play has been suspended by the umpire, one side fails to resume playing within two minutes after the umpire has called "play ball."

(4) If a team employs tactics palpably designed to delay or to hasten the game.

(5) If, after warning by the umpire, any one of the rules of the game is willfully violated.

(6) If the order for the removal of a player is not obeyed within one minute.

(7) If, because of the removal of the players from the game by the umpire or for any cause, there are less than 9 (Fast Pitch) or 10 (Slow Pitch) players on either team.

g. Games that are not considered regulation or regulation tie games, shall be replayed from the beginning. Original line-ups may be changed when the game is replayed.

Sec. 4. The Winner of the Game Shall Be the Team That Scores the Most Runs in a Regulation Game.

a. The score of a called regulation game shall be the score at the end of the last complete inning unless the team second at bat has scored more runs than the first team at bat in the incomplete inning. In this case, the score shall be that of the incomplete inning.

b. The score of a regulation tie game shall be the tie score when the game was terminated. A regulation tie game shall be replayed from the beginning.

c. The score of a forfeited game shall be 7-0 in favor of the team not at fault.

Sec. 5. One Run Shall Be Scored Each Time a Baserunner Legally Touches First, Second, Third Bases, and Home Plate before the Third Out of the Inning.

Sec. 6. A Run Shall Not Be Scored If the Third Out of the Inning Is a Result Of:

a. The batter being put out before legally touching first base.

b. A baserunner being forced out due to the batter becoming a baserunner.

c. (Fast Pitch) A baserunner leaving base before the pitcher releases the ball to the batter. (Slow Pitch) A baserunner leaving base before the pitched ball reaches home plate.

Sec. 7. No Succeeding Runner Shall Score a Run when a Preceding Runner Has Been Declared the Third Out of an Inning.

Sec. 8. A Baserunner Shall Not Score a Run Ahead of the Baserunner Preceding Him in the Batting Order If the Preceding Runner Has Not Been Put Out.

RULE 6. PITCHING REGULATIONS (FAST PITCH)

Sec. 1. The Pitcher Shall Take a Position with Both Feet Firmly on the Ground and in Contact with, but Not off the Side of, the Pitcher's Plate.

a. Preliminary to pitching, the pitcher must come to a full and complete stop facing the batter with the shoulders in line with first and third base, and with the ball held in both hands in front of the body.

b. This position must be maintained at least 2 seconds and not more than 20 seconds before starting the delivery.

c. The pitcher shall not be considered in pitching position unless the catcher is in position to receive the pitch.

d. The pitcher may not take the pitching position on or near the pitcher's plate without having the ball in his possession.

Sec. 2. The Pitch starts when one hand is taken off the ball or the pitcher makes any motion that is part of his wind-up. In the act of delivering the ball, the pitcher shall not take more than one step which must be forward, toward the batter, and simultaneous with the delivery of the ball to the batter. The pivot foot must remain in contact with the pitcher's plate until the other foot with which the pitcher steps toward home plate has touched the ground.

NOTE: It is not a step if the pitcher slides his foot across the pitcher's plate, provided contact is maintained with the pitcher's plate.

Sec. 3. A Legal Delivery Shall Be a Ball Which Is Delivered to the Batter with an Underhand Motion.

a. The release of the ball and the follow-through of the hand and wrist must be forward past the straight line of the body.

b. The hand shall be below the hip and the wrist not farther from the body than the elbow.

c. The pitch is completed with a step toward the batter.

d. The catcher must be within the outside lines of the catcher's box when the pitch is released.

e. The catcher shall return the ball directly to the pitcher after each pitch except after a strike out, or putout made by the catcher. The pitcher has 20 seconds to release the next pitch.

EXCEPTION—Sec. 3e: Does not apply with runners on base.

EFFECT—Sec. 3e: An additional "ball" is awarded to the batter.

Sec. 4. The Pitcher May Use Any Wind-up Desired Providing:

a. He does not make any motion to pitch without immediately delivering the ball to the batter.

b. He does not use a rocker action in which, after having the ball in both hands in pitching position, he removes one hand from the ball, takes a backward and forward swing and returns the ball to both hands in front of the body.

c. He does not use a wind-up in which there is a stop or reversal of the forward motion.

d. He does not make more than one revolution of the arm in the windmill pitch. A pitcher may drop his arm to the side and to the rear before starting the windmill motion.

e. He does not continue to wind-up after taking the forward step which is simultaneous with the release of the ball.

Sec. 5. The Pitcher Shall Not Deliberately Drop, Roll or Bounce the Ball while in Pitching Position in Order to Prevent the Batter from Striking It.

Sec. 6. The Pitcher Shall Not at Any Time During the Game Be Allowed to Use Tape or Other Substance upon the Ball, the Pitching Hand or Fingers. Under the supervision and control of the umpire powdered resin may be used to dry the hands. The pitcher shall not wear a sweatband, bracelet, or similar type item on the wrist or forearm of the pitching arm.

EFFECT—Sec. 1-6: Any infraction of Sections 1 thru 6 is an illegal pitch with the exception of Section 3e which is covered separately. The ball is dead. A ball is called on the batter. Baserunners are entitled to advance one base without liability to be put out. Exception—if the pitcher completes the delivery of the ball to the batter and the batter hits the ball and reaches first base safely and all baserunners advance at least one base then the play stands and the illegal pitch is nullified. A delayed dead ball will be signified by the umpire by extending his left arm horizontally.

NOTE: An illegal pitch shall be called immediately when it becomes illegal. If called by the plate umpire, it shall be called in a voice so that the catcher and the batter will hear it. The plate umpire will also give the delayed dead ball signal. If called by the base umpire, it shall be called so that the nearest fielder shall hear it. The base umpire shall also give the delayed dead ball signal. Failure of players to hear the call shall not void the call.

Sec. 7. At the Beginning of Each Half Inning or when a Pitcher Relieves Another, No More than 1 Minute May Be Used to Deliver No More than 5 Pitches to the Catcher or Other

Teammate. Play shall be suspended during this time. For excessive warm-up pitches a pitcher shall be penalized by awarding a ball to the batter for each pitch in excess of 5.

Sec. 8. The Pitcher Shall Not Throw to a Base while His Foot Is in Contact with the Pitcher's Plate after He Has Taken the Pitching Position.

EFFECT—Sec. 8: Illegal pitch, the ball is dead, a ball is called on the batter, and all runners advance one base. If the throw from the pitcher's plate is during an appeal play, the appeal is cancelled.

NOTE: The pitcher can remove himself from the pitching position by stepping backwards off the pitcher's plate. Stepping forward or sideways constitutes an illegal pitch.

Sec. 9. No Pitch Shall Be Declared When:

a. The pitcher pitches during the suspension of play.

b. The pitcher attempts a quick return of the ball before the batter has taken position or is off balance as a result of a previous pitch.

c. The runner is called out for leaving the base too soon.

d. The pitcher pitches before a baserunner has retouched his base after a foul ball has been declared and the ball is dead.

EFFECT —Sec. 9a-d: The ball is dead and all subsequent action on that pitch is cancelled.

e. NO PLAYER, MANAGER, OR COACH SHALL CALL "TIME" OR EMPLOY ANY OTHER WORD OR PHRASE OR COMMIT ANY ACT WHILE THE BALL IS ALIVE AND IN PLAY FOR THE OBVIOUS PURPOSE OF TRYING TO MAKE THE PITCHER COMMIT AN ILLEGAL PITCH.

EFFECT —Sec. 9e: No pitch shall be declared and a warning issued to the offending team. A repeat of this type act by the team warned shall result in the offender being removed from the game.

Sec. 10. There Shall Be Only One Charged Conference between the Manager or Other Team Representative from the Dugout with Each and Every Pitcher in an Inning. The second charged conference shall result in the removal of the pitcher from the pitching position for the remainder of the game.

Sec. 11. If the Ball Slips from the Pitcher's Hand during His Windup or during the Backswing, the Ball Will Be in Play and the Runners May Advance at Their Own Risk.

RULE 6. PITCHING REGULATIONS (SLOW PITCH)

Sec. 1. The Pitcher Shall Take a Position with One or Both Feet Firmly on the Ground and in Contact with, but Not off the Side of, the Pitcher's Plate. At the time of delivery, both the pivot and the non-pivot foot must be within the length [24 inches (600 mm)] of the pitcher's plate.

a. Preliminary to pitching, the pitcher must come to a full and complete stop facing the batter with the shoulders in line with first and third base, and with the ball held in one or both hands in front of the body.

b. This position must be maintained at least 2 seconds and not more than 20 seconds before starting the delivery.

c. The pitcher shall not be considered in pitching position unless the catcher is in position to receive the pitch.

Sec. 2. The Pitch starts when the pitcher makes any motion that is part of his wind-up after the required pause. Prior to the required pause, any windup may be used. THE PIVOT FOOT MUST REMAIN IN CONTACT WITH THE PITCHER'S PLATE UNTIL THE PITCHED BALL LEAVES THE HAND. It is not necessary to step, but if a step is taken, it must be forward, toward the batter, within the length [24 inches (600 mm)] of the pitcher's plate, and simultaneous with the relaese of the ball.

Sec. 3. A Legal Delivery Shall Be a Ball Which Is Delivered to the Batter with an Underhand Motion.

a. The pitch shall be released at a moderate speed. The speed is left entirely up to the umpire. The umpire shall warn the pitcher who delivers a pitch with excessive speed. If the pitcher repeats such an act after being warned, he shall be removed from the pitcher's position for the remainder of the game.

b. The hand shall be below the hip.

c. The ball must be delivered with a perceptible arch of at least 3 feet (0.99 m) from the time it leaves the pitcher's hand until it reaches home plate. The pitched ball shall not reach a height of more than 12 feet (3.96 m) at its highest point above the ground.

d. The catcher must be within the outside lines of the catcher's box until the pitched ball is batted, or reaches home plate.

e. The catcher shall return the ball directly to the pitcher after each pitch except after a strikeout, or putout made by the catcher. The pitcher has 20 seconds to release the next pitch.

EFFECT—Sec. 3e: An additional "ball" is awarded to the batter.

Sec. 4. The Pitcher May Use Any Wind-up Desired Providing:

a. He does not make any motion to pitch without immediately delivering the ball to the batter.

b. His wind-up is a continuous motion.

c. He does not use a wind-up in which there is a stop or reversal of the forward motion.

d. He delivers the ball toward home plate on the first forward swing of the pitching arm past the hip.

e. He does not continue to wind-up after he releases the ball.

Sec. 5. The Pitcher Shall Not Deliberately Drop, Roll, or Bounce the Ball while in the Pitching Position in Order to Prevent the Batter from Striking It.

Sec. 6. The Pitcher Shall Not at Any Time During the Game Be Allowed to Use Tape or Other Substance upon the Ball, the Pitching Hand, or Fingers. Under the supervision and control of the umpire powdered resin may be used to dry the hands. The pitcher shall not wear a sweatband, bracelet, or similar type item on the wrist or forearm of the pitching arm.

Sec. 7. At the Beginning of Each Half Inning or when a Pitcher Relieves Another, No More than 1 Minute May Be Used to Deliver No More than 5 Pitches to the Catcher or Other Teammate. Play shall be suspended during this time. For excessive warm-up pitches, a pitcher shall be penalized by awarding a ball to the batter for each pitch in excess of 5.

Sec. 8. The Pitcher Shall Not Throw to a Base while His Foot Is in Contact with the Pitcher's Plate after He Has Taken the Pitching Position.

NOTE: The pitcher can remove himself from the pitching position by stepping backwards off the pitcher's plate. Stepping forward or sideways constitutes an illegal pitch.

EFFECT—Sec. 1-8: Any infraction of Sections 1 thru 8 is an illegal pitch. The ball is dead. A ball shall be called on the batter. Baserunners do not advance.

EXCEPTION—If a batter strikes at any illegal pitch it shall be a strike and there shall be no penalty for such an illegal pitch. The ball shall remain in play if hit by the batter. If an illegal pitch is called during an appeal play, the appeal is cancelled.

NOTE: An illegal pitch shall be called immediately when it becomes illegal. If called by the plate umpire, it shall be called in a voice so that the catcher and the batter will hear it. The plate umpire will also give the delayed dead ball signal. If called by the base umpire, it shall be called so that the nearest fielder shall hear it. The base umpire shall also give the delayed dead ball signal. Failure of players to hear the call shall not void the call.

Sec. 9. No Pitch Shall Be Declared When:

a. The pitcher pitches during the suspension of play.

b. The pitcher attempts a quick return of the ball before the batter has taken his position or is off balance as a result of a previous pitch.

c. The runner is called out for leaving the base too soon.

d. The pitcher pitches before the baserunner has retouched his base after a foul ball has been declared and the ball is dead.

e. THE BALL SLIPS FROM THE PITCHER'S HAND DURING HIS WIND-UP OR DURING THE BACKSWING. EFFECT—Sec. 9a-e: The ball is dead and all subsequent action on that pitch is cancelled.

f. NO PLAYER, MANAGER, OR COACH SHALL CALL "TIME" OR EMPLOY ANY OTHER WORD OR PHRASE OR COMMIT ANY ACT WHILE THE BALL IS ALIVE AND IN PLAY FOR THE OBVIOUS PURPOSE OF TRYING TO MAKE THE PITCHER COMMIT AN IL-

LEGAL PITCH.

EFFECT—Sec. 9f: No pitch shall be declared and a warning issued to the offending team. A repeat of this type act by the team warned shall result in the offender being removed from the game.

Sec. 10. There Shall Be Only One Charged Conference between the Manager or Other Team Representative from the Dugout with Each and Every Pitcher in an Inning. The second charged conference shall result in the removal of the pitcher from the pitching position for the remainder of the game.

RULE 7. BATTING

Sec. 1. The Batter Shall Take His Position within the Lines of the Batter's Box.

a. The batter shall not have his entire foot touching the ground completely outside the lines of the batter's box or touching home plate when the ball is hit.

b. The batter shall not step directly across in front of the catcher to the other batter's box while the pitcher is in position ready to pitch.

c. The batter shall not hit the ball with an illegal bat.

EFFECT—Sec. 1a-c: The ball is dead, the batter is out, baserunners may NOT advance.

d. The batter shall not enter the batter's box with an altered bat.

EFFECT—Sec. 1d: The ball is dead, the batter is out, and without warning, the batter is removed from further participation in the game, and baserunners may not advance.

e. The batter must take his position within 1 minute after the umpire has called "play ball."

EFFECT—Sec. 1e: The ball is dead. The batter is out.

Sec. 2. Each Player of the Side at Bat Shall Become a Batter in the Order in Which His Name Appears on the Score Sheet.

a. The batting order of each team must be on the score sheet and must be delivered before the game by the manager or captain to the plate umpire. He shall submit it to the inspection of the manager or captain of the opposing team.

EFFECT—2a: The umpire shall declare a forfeit.

b. The batting order delivered to the umpire must be followed throughout the game unless a player is substituted for another. When this occurs the substitute must take the place of the removed player in the batting order.

c. The first batter in each inning shall be the batter whose name follows that of the last player who completed a turn at bat in the preceding inning.

EFFECT—Sec. 2b-c: Batting out of order is an appeal play which may be made by the defensive team only and while the ball is dead.

(1) If the error is discovered while the incorrect batter is at bat, correct batter may take his place, assume any balls and strikes, and any runs scored or bases run while the incorrect batter was at bat shall be legal.

(2) If the error is discovered after the incorrect batter has completed his turn at bat and before there has been a pitch to another batter, the player who should have batted is out. Any advance or score made because of a ball batted by the improper batter or because of the improper batter's advance to first base on a hit, an error, a base on balls, or a hit batter shall be nullified. The next batter is the player whose name follows that of the player called out for failing to bat. If the batter declared out under these circumstances is the third out, the correct batter in the next inning shall be the player who would have come to bat had the players been put out by ordinary play.

(3) If the error is discovered after the first pitch to the next batter, the turn at bat of the incorrect batter is legal, all runs scored and bases run are legal, and the next batter in order shall be the one whose name follows that of the incorrect batter. No one is called out for failure to bat. Players who have not batted and who have not been called out have lost

their turn at bat until reached again in the regular order.

(4) No baserunner shall be removed from the base he is occupying to bat in his proper place. He merely misses his turn at bat with no penalty. The batter following him in the batting order becomes the legal batter.

d. When the third out in an inning is made before the batter has completed his turn at bat, he shall be the first batter in the next inning, and the ball and strike count on him shall be cancelled.

Sec. 3. The Batter Shall Not Hinder the Catcher from Fielding or Throwing the Ball by Stepping out of the Batter's Box, or Intentionally Hinder the Catcher while Standing within the Batter's Box.

EFFECT—Sec. 3: The ball is dead and baserunners must return to the last base that in the judgment of the umpire was touched at the time of the interference. The batter is out except:

(1) (FP ONLY) If a baserunner attempting to steal is put out, the batter is not also out.

(2) With less than two outs and a runner on third base and the batter interferes with a play being made at home plate, the batter is not out because the runner is out.

Sec. 4. Members of the Team at Bat Shall Not Interfere with a Player Attempting to Field a Foul Fly Ball.

EFFECT—Sec. 4: The ball is dead and the batter is out, and baserunners must return to the base legally held at the time of the pitch.

Sec. 5. The Batter Shall Not Hit a Fair Ball with the Bat a Second Time in Fair Territory.

NOTE: If the batter drops the bat and the ball rolls against the bat in fair territory and, in the umpire's judgment, there was no intention to interfere with the course of the ball, the batter is not out and the ball is alive and in play.

EFFECT—Sec. 5: The ball is dead, the batter is out, and baserunners may not advance.

Sec. 6. A Strike Is Called by the Umpire:

a. (FP ONLY) For each legally pitched ball entering the strike zone before touching the ground and at which the batter does not swing.
EFFECT—Sec. 6a: (FP) The ball is in play

and the baserunners may advance with liability to be put out. The batter is out if:

(1) The catcher does not drop the third strike.

(2) First base is occupied with less than two out.

(SP ONLY) For each legally pitched ball entering the strike zone before touching the ground and at which the batter does not swing. It is not a strike if the pitched ball touches home plate and is not swung at.
EFFECT—Sec. 6a: (SP) The ball is dead.

b. (FP ONLY) For each legally pitched ball struck at and missed by the batter.
EFFECT—Sec. 6b: (FP) The ball is in play and the baserunners may advance with liability to be put out. The batter is out if:

(1) The catcher does not drop the third strike.

(2) First base is occupied with less than two out.

(SP ONLY) For each pitched ball struck at and missed by the batter.
EFFECT—Sec. 6b: (SP) The ball is dead.

c. For each foul tip held by the catcher.
EFFECT—Sec. 6c: (FP) The ball is in play and baserunners may advance with liability to be put out. The batter is out if it is the third strike.
EFFECT—Sec. 6c: (SP) The batter is out if it is the third strike. The ball is dead on any strike.

d. For each foul ball not legally caught on the fly when the batter has less than two strikes.

e. For each pitched ball struck at and missed which touches any part of the batter.

f. When any part of the batter's person is hit with his own batted ball when he is in the batter's box and he has less than two strikes.

g. When a delivered ball by the pitcher hits the batter while the ball is in the strike zone.
EFFECT—Sec. 6d-g: The ball is dead and baserunners must return to their bases without liability to be put out.

Sec. 7. A Ball Is Called by the Umpire:

a. For each pitched ball which does not enter the strike zone or touches the ground before reaching home plate or touches home plate and which is not struck at by the batter.
EFFECT—Sec. 7a: (FP) The ball is in play and baserunners are entitled to advance with

liability to be put out.

EFFECT—Sec. 7a: (SP) The ball is dead. Baserunners may not advance.

b. For each illegally pitched ball.

EFFECT—Sec. 7b: (FP) The ball is dead and baserunners are entitled to advance one base without liability to be put out.

EFFECT—Sec. 7b: (SP) The ball is dead. Baserunners may not advance.

c. (SP ONLY) When a delivered ball by the pitcher hits the batsman outside of the strike zone.

d. When the catcher fails to return the ball directly to the pitcher as required in Rule 6. Section 6.

e. When the pitcher fails to pitch the ball within 20 seconds.

f. For each excessive warm-up pitch.

EFFECT—Sec. 7c-f: The ball is dead. Baserunners may not advance.

Sec. 8. A Fair Ball Is a Legally Batted Ball Which:

a. Settles or is touched on fair ground between home and first base or between home and third base.

b. Bounds past first or third base on or over fair ground.

c. Touches first, second, or third base.

d. While on or over fair ground touches the person or clothing of an umpire or player.

e. First falls on fair ground beyond first or third base. A fair fly must be judged according to the relative position of the ball and the foul line regardless of whether the fielder is on fair or foul ground at the time he touches the ball.

EFFECT—Sec. 8a-e: The ball is in play and baserunners are entitled to advance any number of bases with liability to be put out. The batter becomes a baserunner unless the infield fly rule applies.

f. While on or over fair ground, lands behind a fence or into a stand a distance of more than 225 feet (74.25 m) (Male and Female Fast Pitch), 250 feet (82.5 m) (Female Slow Pitch), or 275 feet (90.75 m) (Male Slow Pitch) from home plate. This is considered a home run. If the distance is less than 225 feet (74.25 m) (Male and Female Fast

Pitch), or 250 feet (82.5 m) (Female Slow Pitch), or 275 (90.75 m) (Male Slow Pitch) from home plate, it is a 2 base hit.

g. Hits a foul line pole on the fly. If the ball hits the pole above the fence level, it shall be a home run.

Sec. 9. A Foul Ball Is a Legally Batted Ball Which:

a. Settles on foul ground between home and first base or between home and third base.

b. Bounds past first or third base on or over foul ground.

c. First touches on foul ground beyond first or third base.

d. While on or over foul ground touches the person or clothing of an umpire, or player, or is blocked.

EFFECT—Sec. 9a-d: (1) The ball is dead unless it is a legally caught foul fly. If a foul fly is caught the batter is out. (2) A strike is called on the batter unless he already had two strikes. (3) Baserunners must return to their bases without liability to be put out unless a foul fly is caught. In this case, the baserunner may advance with liability to be put out after the ball has been touched.

Sec. 10. A Foul Tip Is a Batted Ball Which Goes Directly from the Bat, Not Higher than the Batter's Head, to the Catcher's Hands and Is Legally Caught by the Catcher.

NOTE: It is not a foul tip unless caught and any foul tip that is caught is a strike. In Fast Pitch, the ball is in play, in Slow Pitch, the ball is dead.

EFFECT—Sec. 10 (FP): A strike is called, the ball remains in play and baserunners may advance with liability to be put out.

EFFECT—Sec. 10 (SP): A strike is called, the ball is dead.

Sec. 11. The Batter Is Out under the Following Circumstances:

a. When the third strike is struck at and missed and touches any part of the batter's person.

b. When a batter appears in the batter's box with, or is discovered using, an altered bat.

c. When a fly ball is legally caught.

d. Immediately when he hits an infield fly with baserunners on first and second—or on first, second, and third—with less than two out.

This is called the infield fly rule.

e. The batter is out if a fielder intentionally drops a fair fly ball (including a line drive) (FP or SP) or a bunt (FP ONLY) which can be caught by an infielder, with ordinary effort, with 1st, 1st and 2nd, 1st and 3rd, or 1st, 2nd, and 3rd base occupied with less than 2 outs.
NOTE: A trapped ball shall not be considered as having been intentionally dropped.
EFFECT—Sec. 11e: The ball is dead, and baserunners must return to the last base touched at the time of the pitch.

f. The batter-runner is out if a preceding runner who is not yet out, and in the umpire's judgment, intentionally interferes with a fielder who is attempting to catch a thrown ball or to throw a ball in an attempt to complete the play. The runner shall also be called out and interference called.

g. (FP ONLY) When the third strike is caught by the catcher.

h. (FP ONLY) When he has 3 strikes if there are less than 2 outs and first base is occupied.

i. (FP ONLY) When he bunts foul after the second strike. If the ball is caught in the air, it remains alive and in play.

j. (SP ONLY) When a third strike is called.

k. (SP ONLY) When he bunts or chops the ball downward.

Sec. 12. The Batter Is Not Out If a Fielder Making a Play on Him Uses an Illegal Glove. The manager of the offended team has the option of having the batter bat over and assuming the ball and strike count he had prior to the pitch he hit, or taking the result of the play.

Sec. 13. On Deck Batter.

a. The on deck batter is the offensive player whose name follows the name of the batter in the batting order.

b. The on deck batter shall take a position within the lines of the on deck circle.

c. The on deck batter may leave the on deck circle:
(1) When he becomes the batter.
(2) To direct baserunners advancing from third to home plate.

d. When the on deck batter interferes with the defensive player's opportunity to make a play on a runner, the runner closest to home plate at the time of the interference shall be declared out.

e. The provision of Rule 7, Section 4, shall apply to the on deck batter.

RULE 8. BASERUNNING

Sec. 1. The Baserunners Must Touch Bases in Legal Order, I.E., First, Second, Third, and Home Plate.

a. When a baserunner must return while the ball is in play, he must touch the bases in reverse order.
EFFECT—Sec. 1a: The ball is in play and baserunners must return with liability to be put out.

b. When a baserunner acquires the right to a base by touching it before being put out he is entitled to hold the base until he has legally touched the next base in order or is forced to vacate it for a succeeding baserunner.

c. When a baserunner dislodges a base from its proper position neither he nor succeeding runners in the same series of plays are compelled to follow a base unreasonably out of position.
EFFECT—Sec. 1b-c: The ball is in play and baserunners may advance with liability to be put out.

d. A baserunner shall not run bases in reverse order either to confuse the fielders or to make a travesty of the game.
EFFECT—Sec. 1d: The ball is dead and the baserunner is out.

e. Two baserunners may not occupy the same base simultaneously.
EFFECT—Sec. 1e: The runner who first legally occupied the base shall be entitled to it: the other baserunner may be put out by being touched with the ball.

f. Failure of a **preceding** runner to touch a base, or to leave a base legally on a caught fly ball and who is declared out does not affect the status of a **succeeding** baserunner who touches bases in proper order. However, if the failure to touch a base in regular order or to leave a base legally on a caught fly ball, is the third out of the inning **no succeeding** runner may score a run.

g. No runner may return to touch a missed base, or one he had left illegally, after a following runner has scored. After the ball becomes dead, no runner may return to touch a missed base or one he has left after he has advanced to and touched a base beyond the missed base or one he has left illegally, even after the ball becomes alive.

h. No runner may return to touch a missed base or one he had left illegally, once he enters his team area.

i. When a walk is issued, all runners must touch all bases in legal order.

j. Bases left too soon on a caught fly ball must be retouched while in route to awarded bases.

k. Awarded bases must also be touched and in proper order.

Sec. 2. The Batter Becomes a Baserunner.

a. As soon as he hits a fair ball.
    EFFECT—Sec. 2a: The ball is in play and the batter becomes a baserunner with liability to be put out.

b. (FP ONLY) When the catcher fails to catch the third strike before the ball touches the ground when there are less than two outs and first base is unoccupied, or anytime there are two outs. This is called the third strike rule.

c. When a fair ball strikes the person or clothing of an umpire on foul ground.
    EFFECT—Sec. 2b-c: The ball is in play and the batter becomes a baserunner with liability to be put out.

d. When four balls have been called by the umpire.
    EFFECT—Sec. 2d: (FP) The ball is in play unless it has been blocked. The batter is entitled to one base without liability to be put out.
    EFFECT—Sec. 2d: (SP) The ball is dead. Baserunners may not advance unless forced. If the pitcher desires to walk a batter intentionally he may do so by notifying the plate umpire, who shall award the batter first base.

e. When the catcher or any other fielder interferes with or prevents him from striking at a pitched ball.

EFFECT—Sec. 2e: The ball is dead and not in play and the batter is entitled to one base without liability to be put out unless the batter reaches first base safely and all other runners have advanced at least one base then play continues without reference to the interference.

f. When a fair ball strikes the person or clothing of the umpire or a baserunner on fair ground.
    EFFECT—Sec. 2f: (1) If the ball hits the umpire or baserunner after passing a fielder other than the pitcher or is touched by infielder including the pitcher the ball is in play: (2) If the ball hits the umpire or baserunner before passing a fielder, the ball is dead and the batter is entitled to first base without liability to be put out.

g. (FP ONLY) When a pitched ball not struck at touches any part of the batter's person or clothing while he is in the batter's box. It does not matter if the ball strikes the ground before hitting him. The batter's hands are not to be considered as part of the bat.
    EFFECT—Sec. 2g: The ball is dead and the batter is entitled to one base without liability to be put out unless he made no effort to avoid being hit. In this case, the plate umpire calls either a ball or a strike.

Sec. 3. Baserunners Are Entitled to Advance with Liability to be Put Out under the Following Circumstances:

a. (FP ONLY) When a ball leaves the pitcher's hand on a pitch.

b. When the ball is overthrown into fair or foul territory and is not blocked.

c. When the ball is batted into fair territory and is not blocked.

d. When a legally caught fly ball is first touched.

e. If a fair ball strikes the umpire or a baserunner after having passed an infielder, other than the pitcher or having been touched by an infielder, including the pitcher, the ball shall be considered in play. Also, if a fair ball strikes an umpire on foul ground, the ball shall be in play.
    EFFECT—Sec. 3a-e: The ball is alive and in play.

Sec. 4. A Player Forfeits His Exemption from Liability to Get Put Out:

a. If while the ball is in play he fails to touch

the base to which he was entitled before attempting to make the next base. If the runner put out, is the batter-baserunner at first base or any other baserunner forced to advance because the batter became a baserunner, this out is a force-out.

b. If after overrunning first base, the batter-baserunner attempts to continue to second base.

c. If after dislodging the base, the batter-baserunner tries to continue to the next base.

Sec. 5. Baserunners Are Entitled to Advance without Liability to Be Put Out:

a. When forced to vacate a base because the batter was awarded a base on balls.
EFFECT—Sec. 5a: (FP) The ball remains in play unless it is blocked. Baserunner affected is entitled to one base and may advance farther at his own risk if the ball is in play.
EFFECT—Sec. 5a: (SP) The ball is dead.

b. When a fielder obstructs the baserunner from making a base unless the fielder is trying to field a batted ball or has the ball ready to touch the baserunner.
EFFECT—Sec. 5b: When obstruction occurs, the umpire shall call and signal "Obstruction."
(1) If a play is being made on the obstructed runner, or if the batter-runner is obstructed before he touches first base, the ball is dead and all runners shall advance, without liability to be put out, to the bases they would have reached, in the umpires's judgment, if there had been no obstruction. The obstructed runner shall be awarded at least one base beyond the base he had last legally touched before the obstruction. Any preceding runners, forced to advance by the award of bases as the penalty for obstruction, shall advance without liability to be put out.
(2) If no play is being made on the obstructed runner, the play shall proceed until no further action is possible. The umpire shall then call "TIME" and impose such penalties, if any, as in his judgment will nullify the act of obstruction.

c. (FP ONLY) When a wild pitch or passed ball goes under, over, through, or lodges in the backstop.
EFFECT—Sec. 5c: The ball is dead. All baserunners are awarded one base only. The batter is awarded first base only on the fourth ball.

d. When forced to vacate a base because the batter was awarded a base.
(1) (FP ONLY) For being hit by a pitched ball.
(2) For being interfered with by the catcher when striking at a pitched ball.
(3) (FP ONLY) If, with a runner on third base and trying to score by means of a squeeze play or a steal, the catcher or any oher fielder steps on, or in front of home plate without possession of the ball, or touches the batter or his bat, the pitcher shall be charged with an illegal pitch, the batter shall be awarded first base on the interference and the ball is dead.
EFFECT—Sec. 5d: (1)-(3): The ball is dead and baserunners may not advance farther than the base to which they are entitled.

e. (FP ONLY) When a pitcher makes an illegal pitch.
EFFECT—Sec. 5e: The ball is dead and baserunners may advance to the base to which they are entitled without liability to be put out.

f. When a fielder contacts or catches a fair batted or thrown ball with his cap, mask, glove, or any part of his uniform while it is detached from its proper place on his person.
EFFECT—Sec. 5f: The baserunners shall be entitled to 3 bases if a batted ball, or 2 bases if a thrown ball, and in either case the baserunners may advance farther at their own risk. If the illegal catch or touch is made on a fair hit ball, which in the opinion of the umpire, would have cleared the outfield fence in flight, the runner shall be awarded a home run.

g. When the ball is in play and is overthrown into foul territory and is blocked.
EFFECT—Sec. 5g: The ball is dead. In all cases where a thrown ball goes into a stand for spectators or over, through, or under any fence surrounding the playing field, or

hits any person or object not engaged in the game, or into the player's benches (including bats lying near such benches), whether the ball rebounds into the playing field or not, or remains in the meshes of any wire screen protecting the spectators, each and every baserunner shall be awarded 2 bases. When a first throw is made by an infielder, the umpire in awarding such bases shall be governed by the position of each runner at the time the ball was delivered by the pitcher: when the throw is made by an outfielder or is the result of any succeeding play or attempted play; the award shall be governed by the position of each runner and the last base he has touched at the time the final throw was made. In Fast Pitch only, when the throw is made by the catcher on a ball not hit, the award shall be governed by the position of each runner and the last base he has touched at the time of the throw. When a fielder loses possession of the ball such as on an attempted tag, and the ball then enters the dead ball area or becomes blocked, all runners are awarded 1 base from the last base touched at the time the ball entered the dead ball area or became blocked.

NOTE: If all runners, including the batter-runner, have advanced at least 1 base when an infielder makes a wild throw on the first play after the pitch, the award shall be governed by the position of the runners when the wild throw was made.

h. When a fair-batted fly ball goes over the fence or into the stands it shall entitle the batter to a home run unless it passes out of the grounds or into a distance less than 225 feet (74.25 m) (Male and Female Fast Pitch), 250 feet (82.5) (Female Slow Pitch), or 275 feet (90.75 m) (Male Slow Pitch) from home plate, in which case the batter shall be entitled to 2 bases only. The batter must touch the bases in regular order. The point at which the fence or stand is less than 225 feet (74.25 m) (Male and Female Fast Pitch), 250 feet (82.5 m) (Female Slow Pitch), or 275 feet (90.75 m) (Male Slow Pitch) from home plate shall be plainly indicated for the umpire's guidance.

i. When a fair ball bounds or rolls into a stand, over, under, or through a fence or other obstruction marking the boundaries of the playing field.
EFFECT—Sec. 5i: The ball is dead and all baserunners are awarded 2 bases, from time of pitch.

j. When a legally caught ball in playable territory is carried by the fielder unintentionally into dead ball territory, the ball is dead, the batter is out and all runners advance 1 base beyond the base they occupied at the time of the pitch. If, in the judgment of the umpire, the fielder INTENTIONALLY carries a legally caught fly ball into dead ball territory, the ball is dead, the batter is out and all runners are awarded 2 bases beyond the base they occupied at the time of the pitch.

Sec. 6. A Baserunner Must Return to His Base under the Following Circumstances:

a. When a foul ball is illegally caught and is so declared by the umpire.

b. When an illegally batted ball is declared by the umpire.

c. When a batter or baserunner is called out for interference. Other baserunners shall return to the last base which was in the judgment of the umpire legally touched by him at the time of the interference.

d. (FP ONLY) When there is interference by the plate umpire or his clothing with the catcher's attempt to throw.

e. When any part of the batter's person is touched by a pitched ball swung at and missed.

f. When a batter is hit by a pitched ball, unless forced.

g. When a foul ball is not caught.
EFFECT—Sec. 6a-g: (1) The ball is dead. (2) The baserunners must return to base without liability to be put out except when forced to go to the next base because the batter became a baserunner. (3) No runs shall score unless all bases are occupied. (4) Baserunners need not touch the intervening bases in returning to base but must return promptly. (5) However, they must be allowed sufficient time to return.

h. (SP ONLY) Base Stealing. Under no conditions is a runner permitted to steal a base when a pitched ball is not batted. The runner must return to his base.
EFFECT—Sec. 6h: Baserunners may leave

their base when a pitched ball is batted or reaches home plate, but must return to that base immediately after each pitch not hit by the batter.

i. When a caught fair fly ball (including a line drive) (FP and SP) or bunt (FP ·ONLY) which can be caught by an infielder with ordinary effort is intentionally dropped with less than 2 outs, with a runner on 1st base, 1st and 2nd, 1st and 3rd, or 1st, 2nd, and 3rd base.

Sec. 7. Batter-Baserunners Are Out under the Following Circumstances:

a. (FP ONLY) When the catcher drops the third strike and he is legally touched with the ball by a fielder before touching first base.

b. (FP ONLY) When the catcher drops the third strike and the ball is held on first base before the batter-runner reaches first base.

c. When after a fair ball is hit, he is legally touched with the ball before he touches first base.

d. When after a fair ball, the ball is held by a fielder touching first base with any part of his person before the batter-baserunner touches first base.

e. When after a fly ball, the ball is caught by a fielder before it touches the ground or any object other than a fielder.

f. When after a fair ball is hit or a base on balls is issued, or when the batter may legally advance to 1st base on a dropped 3rd strike (FP ONLY), he fails to advance to 1st base and instead enters his team area.
EFFECT—Sec. 7a-f: The ball is in play and the batter-baserunner is out.

g. When he runs outside the 3-foot (0.99 m) line and in the opinion of the umpire interferes with the fielder taking the throw at first base. However, he may run outside the 3-foot (0.99 m) line to avoid a fielder attempting to field a batted ball.

h. When he interferes with a fielder attempting to field a batted ball or intentionally interferes with a thrown ball. If this interference, in the judgment of the umpire, is an obvious attempt to prevent a double play, the baserunner closest to home plate shall also be called out.

i. When a batter-baserunner interferes with a play at home plate in an attempt to prevent an obvious out at the plate. The runner is also out.
EFFECT—Sec. 7g-i: The ball is dead and the batter-baserunner is out.

Sec. 8. The Baserunner Is Out:

a. When in running to any base, he runs more than 3 feet (0.99 m) from a direct line between a base and the next one in regular or reverse order to avoid being touched by the ball in the hand of a fielder.

b. When, while the ball is in play, he is legally touched with the ball in the hand of a fielder while not in contact with a base.

c. When on a force-out a fielder tags him with the ball or holds the ball on the base to which the baserunner is forced to advance before the runner reaches the base.

d. When the baserunner fails to return to touch the base he previously occupied when play is resumed after suspension of play.

e. When a baserunner physically passes a preceding baserunner before that runner has been put out.
EFFECT—Sec. 8a-e: The ball is in play and the baserunner is out.

f. When the baserunner leaves his base to advance to another base before a caught fly ball has touched a fielder, provided the ball is returned to a fielder and legally held on that base or a fielder legally touches the baserunner before the baserunner returns to his base.

g. When the baserunner fails to touch the intervening base or bases in regular or reverse order and the ball is in play and legally held on that base, or the baserunner is legally touched while off the base that he missed.

h. When the batter-runner legally overruns first base, attempts to run to second base and is legally touched while off base.

i. In running or sliding for home base, he fails to touch home base and makes no attempt to return to the base, when a fielder holds the ball in his hand while touching home base, and appeals to the umpire for the decision.
EFFECT—Sec. 8f-i: (1) These are appeal plays and the defensive team loses the privilege of putting the baserunner out if the appeal is not made before the next pitch,

legal or illegal. (2) The ball is in play and the baserunner is out.

NOTE: On appeal plays, the appeal must be made before the next pitch, legal or illegal, or before the defensive team has left the field. The defensive team has "left the field" when the pitcher and all infielders have clearly left their normal fielding positions and have left fair territory on their way to the bench or dugout area. (3) Baserunners may leave their base on appeal plays when:

    (a) (FP ONLY) The ball leaves the 8 foot (2.64 m) circle around the pitcher's plate or when the ball leaves the pitcher's possession.

    (b) (SP ONLY) The defensive team makes known their intent to appeal or the pitcher steps backwards off the pitcher's plate or throws the ball while off the pitcher's plate and after the umpire declares "Play Ball."

j. When the baserunner interferes with a fielder attempting to field a batted ball or intentionally interferes with a thrown ball. If this interference, in the judgment of the umpire, is an obvious attempt to prevent a double play, the immediate succeeding runner shall also be called out.

k. When a baserunner is struck with a fair batted ball while off base and before it passes an infielder excluding the pitcher.

l. When a runner intentionally kicks a ball which an infielder has missed.

m. When a baserunner on third base the batter interferes with a play being made at home plate with less than 2 outs.

n. When in the judgment of the umpire, the base coach at third base or first base, touches or holds the runner, physically to assist this runner in returning to or leaving third or first base. The runner is not out if a play is not being made on him.

o. When the coach near third base runs in the direction of home plate on or near the baseline while a fielder is attempting to make a play on a batted or thrown ball and thereby draws a throw to home plate. The baserunner nearest to third base shall be declared out.

p. When one or more members of the offensive team stand or collect at or around a base to which a baserunner is advancing thereby confusing the fielders and adding to the difficulty of making the play.

NOTE: Sec. 8p: Members of a team include bat boy or any other person authorized to sit on team's bench.

q. When the baserunner runs the bases in reverse order, to confuse the defensive team or to make a farce out of the game. This includes the batter-runner moving back toward home plate to avoid or delay a tag by a fielder.

r. If coach intentionally interferes with a thrown ball. When a runner, after being declared out or after scoring, interferes with a defensive player's opportunity to make a play on another runner, the runner closest to home plate at the time of the interference, shall be declared out.

EFFECT—Sec. 8j-r: The ball is dead and the baserunner is out. No bases may be run unless necessitated by the batter becoming a baserunner.

s. (FP ONLY) When the baserunner fails to keep contact with the base to which he is entitled until a legally pitched ball has been released. When a baserunner is legitimately off his base after a pitch or the result of a batter completing his turn at bat, while the pitcher has the ball within an 8 foot (2.64 m) radius of the pitcher's plate, he must immediately attempt to advance to the next base or immediately return to his base.

(1) Failure to immediately proceed to the next base or return to his base, once the pitcher has the ball within the 8 foot (2.64 m) radius of the pitcher's plate, shall result in the baserunner being declared out.

(2) Once the runner returns to a base, for any reason, he shall be declared out if he leaves said base unless a play is made on him or another runner; or the pitcher does not have the ball in the 8 foot (2.64 m) radius; or the pitcher released the ball to the batter.

NOTE: A base on balls or dropped 3rd strike, in which the runner is entitled to run, is treated the same as a batted ball. The batter-runner may continue past first base, and is entitled to run toward second base, as long as he does not stop at first base. If he stops after he rounds first base, he then must comply with Section 8s (1).

t. (SP ONLY) When the baserunner fails to keep contact with the base to which he is entitled, until a legally pitched ball has reached home plate.

EFFECT—Sec. 8s-t: The ball is dead. NO PITCH is declared and the baserunner is out.

Sec. 9. Baserunners Are Not Out under the Following Circumstances:

a. When a baserunner runs behind the fielder and outside the baseline in order to avoid interfering with a fielder attempting to field the ball in the base path.

b. When a baserunner does not run in a direct line to the base providing the fielder in the direct line does not have the ball in his possession.

c. When more than one fielder attempts to field a batted ball and the baserunner comes in contact with the one who, in the umpire's judgment was not entitled to field the ball.

d. When a baserunner is hit with a fair batted ball that has passed through an infielder, excluding the pitcher, and in the umpire's judgment no other infielder had a chance to play the ball.

e. When a baserunner is touched with a ball not securely held by a fielder.

f. When the defensive team does not request the umpire's decision on an appeal play until after the next pitch.

g. When the batter-runner overruns first base after touching it and returning directly to the base.

h. When the baserunner is not given sufficient time to return to a base, he shall not be called out for being off base before the pitcher releases the ball. He may advance as though he had left the base legally.

i. A runner who has legally started to advance cannot be stopped by the pitcher receiving the ball while on the pitching plate nor by stepping on the plate with the ball in his possession.

j. When a baserunner holds his base until a fly ball touches a fielder and then attempts to advance.

k. When hit by a batted ball when touching their base, unless they intentionally interfere with the ball or a fielder making a play.

l. When a baserunner slides into a base and dislodges it from its proper position, the base is considered to have followed the runner.

EFFECT—Sec. 9l: A baserunner having made such a base safely shall not be out for being off that base. He may return to that base without liability to be put out when the base has been replaced. A runner forfeits this exemption if he attempts to advance beyond the dislodged base before it is again in proper position.

m. When a fielder makes a play on a runner while using an illegal glove. The manager of the offended team has the option of having the entire play, including the batter's turn at bat, nullified, with the batter batting over, assuming the ball and strike count he had before he hit the ball and runners returned to their original bases which they held prior to the batted ball or taking the result of the play.

n. When the baserunner is hit by a fair batted ball, after it is touched or touches any fielder, including the pitcher.

RULE 9. DEAD BALL—BALL IN PLAY

Sec. 1. The Ball Is Dead and Not in Play in the Following Circumstances:

a. When the ball is batted illegally.

b. When the batter steps from one box to another when the pitcher is ready to pitch.

c. When a ball is pitched illegally.

EXCEPTION—Sec. 1c: (FP) If the pitcher completes the delivery of the ball to the batter and the batter hits the ball, reaches first safely, and all baserunners advance at least one base, then the play stands and the pitch is no longer illegal.

EXCEPTION—Sec. 1c: (SP) If the batter swings at an illegal pitch, the play stands and the pitch is no longer illegal.

d. When "No Pitch" is declared.

e. When a pitched ball touches any part of the

batter's person or clothing whether the ball is struck at or not.

f.   When a foul ball is not caught.

g.   When a baserunner is called out for leaving the base too soon on a pitched ball.

h.   When the offensive team causes an interference.

   (1) When a batter intentionally strikes the ball a second time, strikes it with a thrown bat, or deflects its course in any way while running to first base.

   (2) When an overthrow is intentionally touched by a coach.

   (3) When a fair ball strikes a baserunner or umpire before touching an infielder including the pitcher or before passing an infielder other than the pitcher.

   (4) When the batter interferes with the catcher.

   (5) When a member of the offensive team interferes intentionally with a live ball.

   (6) When a runner intentionally kicks a ball which a fielder has missed.

   (7) (FP ONLY) When, with a baserunner on third base, the batter interferes with the play being made at home plate with less than two outs.

i.   The ball shall not be playable outside the established limits of the playing field.

j.   If an accident to a runner is such as to prevent him from proceeding to a base to which he is awarded, a substitute runner shall be permitted for the injured player.

k.   In case of interference with batter or fielder.

l.   (FP ONLY) When the batter bunts or chops the pitched ball.

m.   (FP ONLY) When a wild pitch or passed ball goes under, over, or through the backstop.

n.   When time is called by the umpire.

o.   When any part of the batter's person is hit with his own batted ball when he is in the batter's box.

p.   When a baserunner runs bases in reverse order either to confuse the fielders or to make a travesty of the game.

q.   When the batter is hit by a pitched ball.

r.   When in the judgment of the umpire, the coach touches or helps the runner physically to assist him to return or to leave a base or when the coach near third base runs in the direction of home plate on or near the baseline while the fielder is attempting to make a play on a batted or thrown ball and thereby draws a throw to home plate.

s.   (FP ONLY) When there is interference by the plate umpire or his clothing with the catcher's attempt to throw.

t.   When one or more members of the offensive team stand or collect at or around a base to which a baserunner is advancing, thereby confusing the fielders and adding to the difficulty of making a play.

u.   (FP ONLY) When the baserunner fails to keep contact with the base to which he is entitled, until a legally pitched ball has been released.

v.   (SP ONLY) When a baserunner fails to keep contact with the base to which he is entitled, until a legally pitched ball has reached home plate.

w.   When a play is being made on an obstructed runner or if the batter-runner is obstructed before he touches first base.

x.   (SP ONLY) After each strike or ball.

y.   When the catcher interferes with the batter's attempt to hit a pitch.
   EXCEPTION—Sec. 1y: The ball remains alive if the batter reaches first base safely and all other runners have advanced at least one base.

z.   When a blocked ball is declared.

aa.   When a batter enters the batter's box with or uses an altered bat.

ab.   When a batter hits a ball with an illegal bat.

ac.   When a caught fair fly ball (including a line drive) (FP and SP) or bunt (FP ONLY) which can be handled by an infielder with ordinary effort is intentionally dropped with less than 2 outs and a runner on 1st base, 1st and 2nd, 1st and 3rd, or 1st, 2nd, and 3rd bases.

ad.   When a fielder intentionally carries a legally caught fly ball into dead ball territory.
   EFFECT—Sec. 1a-1ad: Baserunners cannot advance on a dead ball, unless forced to do so by reason of the batter having reached first base as entitled to or they are awarded a base or bases.

Sec. 2. The ball Is in Play in the Following Circumstances:

a.   At the start of the game and each half

inning when the pitcher has the ball while standing in his pitching position and the plate umpire has called "Play Ball."

b. When the ball becomes dead, it shall be put in play when the pitcher is within 8 feet (2.64 m) of the pitcher's plate with the ball and the plate umpire calls "Play Ball."

c. When the infield fly rule is enforced.

d. When a thrown ball goes past a fielder and remains in playable territory.

e. When a fair ball strikes an umpire or baserunner on fair ground after passing or touching an infielder.

f. When a fair ball strikes an umpire on foul ground.

g. When the baserunners have reached the bases to which they are entitled when the fielder illegally fields a batted or thrown ball.

h. When a baserunner is called out for passing a preceding runner.

i. When no play is being made on an obstructed runner, the ball shall remain alive until the play is over.

j. When a fair ball is legally batted.

k. When a baserunner must return in reverse order while the ball is in play.

l. When a baserunner acquires the right to a base by touching it before being put out.

m. When a base is dislodged while baserunners are progressing around the bases.

n. When a baserunner runs more than 3 feet (0.99 m) from a direct line between a base and the next one in regular or reverse order to avoid being touched by the ball in the hand of a fielder.

o. When a baserunner is tagged or forced out.

p. When the umpire calls the baserunner out for failure to return and touch the base when play is resumed after a suspension of play.

q. When an appeal play is enforced and involved.

r. When the batter hits the ball.

s. When a live ball strikes a photographer, groundskeeper, policeman, etc., assigned to the game.

t. When a fly ball has been legally caught.

u. When a thrown ball goes into foul territory and is neithj blocked nor obstructed.

v. When a thrown ball strikes an offensive player.

w. If the batter drops the bat and the ball rolls against the bat in fair territory and, in the umpire's judgment, there was no intention to interfere with the course of the ball. The batter is not out and the ball is alive and in play.

x. When a thrown ball strikes an umpire.

y. Whenever the ball is not dead as provided in Section 1 of this rule.

z. When a thrown ball strikes a coach.

aa. (FP ONLY) When a ball has been called on the batter and when four balls have been called but the batter may not be put out before he reaches first base.

ab. (FP ONLY) When a strike has been called on the batter and when three strikes have been called on the batter.

ac. (FP ONLY) When a foul tip has been legally caught.

ad. (SP ONLY) As long as there is a play as a result of the hit by the batter. This includes a subsequent appeal play.

ae. (FP ONLY) If the ball slips from a pitcher's hand during his wind-up or during the backswing.

Sec. 3 (SP ONLY) The Ball Remains Alive until the Umpire Calls "Time" Which Should Be Done when the Ball Is Held by a Player in the Infield Area and, in the Opinion of the Umpire, All Play Has Ceased.

OFFICIAL DIMENSIONS of softball diamonds.

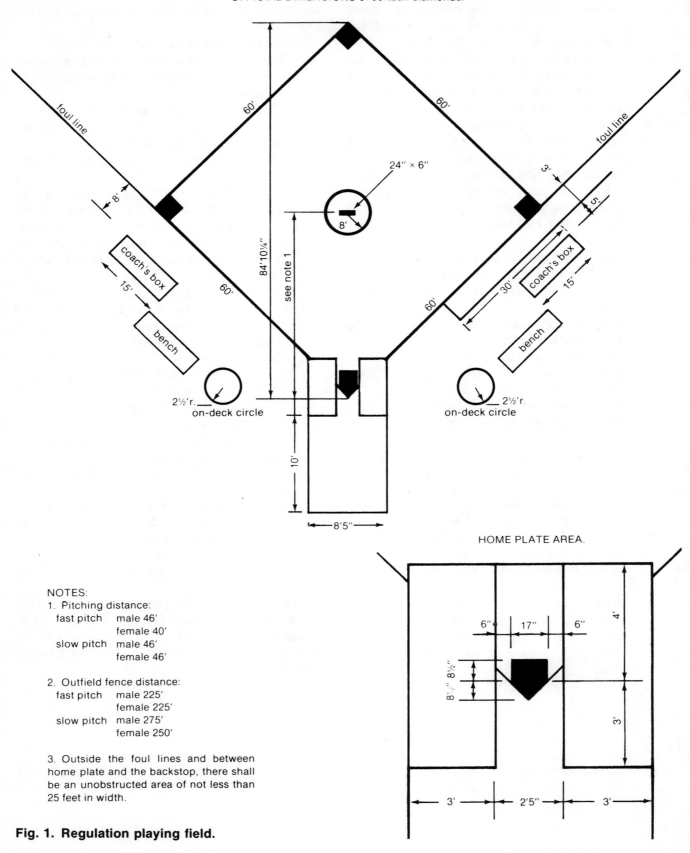

NOTES:
1. Pitching distance:
    fast pitch   male 46'
                       female 40'
    slow pitch   male 46'
                       female 46'

2. Outfield fence distance:
    fast pitch   male 225'
                       female 225'
    slow pitch   male 275'
                       female 250'

3. Outside the foul lines and between home plate and the backstop, there shall be an unobstructed area of not less than 25 feet in width.

Fig. 1. Regulation playing field.

HOME PLATE AREA.

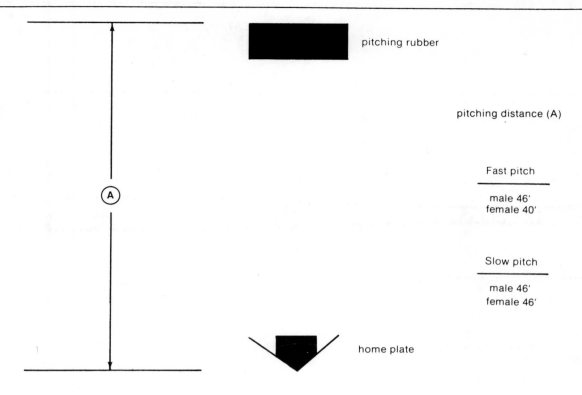

Fig. 2. Regulation pitching distances.

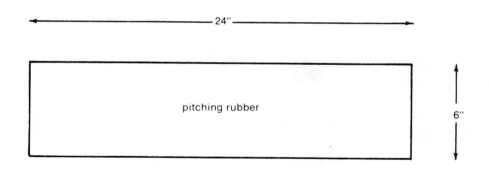

PITCHING RUBBER shall be made of wood or rubber.

Fig. 3. Official pitching rubber.

OFFICIAL BAT SPECIFICATIONS.

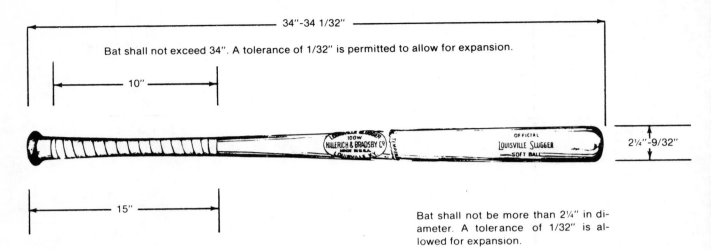

34″–34 1/32″

Bat shall not exceed 34″. A tolerance of 1/32″ is permitted to allow for expansion.

10″

2¼″–9/32″

15″

Bat shall not be more than 2¼″ in diameter. A tolerance of 1/32″ is allowed for expansion.

Safety grip shall be no less than 10″ long. It shall not extend more than 15″ from small end of bat.

Fig. 4. Official softball bat.

Fig. 5. Official softball.

Glossary

Assist—a play in which two or more players handle the ball to complete the putout.

Back up—a position taken by one fielder behind another in case the ball gets past the first fielder.

Bad hop—an unusual or tricky bounce of a batted or thrown ball.

Bag—another term for base.

"Ball"—a pitch not struck at by the batter that fails to fall in the strike zone (see rules for strike zone).

Baseline—the marked or imaginary line between the bases.

Batter's box—the area to which the batter is restricted while in position to hit a pitched ball.

Batting practice—the period of time allowed for players to practice hitting before a game.

Batting slump—the period of time when a hitter's batting average drops below his or her normal average.

Batting stance—the position taken by a batter awaiting a pitched ball.

Blocking the plate—taking the tag in crouch position, usually a move by the catcher, to keep a runner from scoring a run at home plate. Glove hand is in front of the plate and on the ground.

Breaking pitch—the movement of a pitched ball from a straight line; that is, the break of a curve.

Chance—another term for making a play.

Change-up—a pitch that is intentionally slowed up from normal pitching speed.

Clean catch—a catch made by a fielder without bobbling or juggling the ball.

Chopper—a high-bouncing batted ball.

Chucker—the pitcher.

Closed stance—a type of stance, with front foot closer to the plate, taken by the hitter as he waits for the pitch.

Covering a base—moving to a base to take the throw for a putout.

Curve—a pitched ball that moves in a curving line rather than a straight line.

Cut-off man—a player, usually an infielder, who intentionally intercepts a throw instead of allowing the ball to go where it was originally intended.

Double—a two-base hit.

Double play—a play by the defensive team in which two offensive players are legally put out in one continuous play.

Double steal—a play in which two offensive players each steal a base on a continuous play.

Dropped third strike—a failure by the catcher to hold on to the ball on a third strike. Batter can run and try to reach first on this play.

Error—a mistake by a defensive player.

Extra-base hit—a base hit where the hitter gets more than one base.

First sacker—the first baseman.

Fly ball—a batted ball hit into the air.

Follow-through—the act of continuing a motion in throwing or hitting.

Force-out—an out that can be made only when a baserunner loses the right to the base he is occupying because the batter becomes a baserunner and before the batter or a succeeding baserunner has been put out. (No tag is needed.)

Foul line—the lines that enclose the field from home plate to the outfield.

Foul tip—a batted ball that goes directly from the bat, not higher than the batter's head, into the catcher's hands.

Glove—equipment used by infielders as an aid in catching the ball. A glove has five finger placements.

Ground ball—a batted ball that rolls along the ground.

Grounder—a ground ball.

Hit and run—an offensive play in which the baserunner leaves with the pitch. The second baseman moves to cover second, and the hitter then tries to hit the ball through the hole left by the second baseman.

Hit away—a situation in which the batter is swinging for a hit and not bunting.

Home run—a base hit that enables the batter either to hit the ball fairly over the outfield fence or circle the bases on a hit that does not go over the fence.

Hook slide—a sliding action performed by the baserunner to avoid a tag. The bag is hooked with the toe.

Infielder—the first baseman, second baseman, third baseman, or shortstop. Pitchers and catchers are also considered infielders.

In-shoot—a type of pitch that breaks in toward the batter, sometimes referred to as a screwball.

Inside pitch—a pitched ball that either fails to pass over the plate or barely passes over the batter's side of the plate.

Keystone sack—second base.

Let-up—a change-up or slow ball.

Line drive—a batted ball that stays on a straight line instead of going high into the air or onto the ground.

Mask—safety equipment that straps around the catcher's head and serves as a protective covering for the face.

Mitt—playing equipment similar to a glove, except that the thumb portion is separated from the other part of the mitt. Only the first baseman and the catcher may wear a mitt.

On-deck circle—a marked circle in foul territory where the next batter in the lineup awaits his turn to hit.

On-deck hitter—the next batter in the lineup waiting to bat.

Open stance—a type of stance a batter assumes with the front foot farther from the plate than the rear foot as he awaits the pitch.

Opposite field hitter—a batter who usually hits the ball to the opposite field from where it's expected; that is, most right-handed hitters hit the ball to left field and most left-handed hitters hit the ball to right field.

Outfielder—a player who normally plays an outfield position—left, right, or center field.

Outside pitch—a pitched ball that either fails to pass over that portion of the plate farthest from the batter or just barely passes over it.

Pick-off play—a defensive play usually started by the catcher to catch a runner off base.

Pinch hitter—a batter who is substituted for another batter already in the game.

Pitching rubber—the wood or rubber rectangle on which the pitcher stands to pitch the ball.

Pivot foot—the foot on which body weight is shifted. Also, the foot a pitcher must keep in contact with the pitcher's plate until the ball is released.

Play deep—plays farther back—the position taken by either an infielder or outfielder in backing up from normal position.

Pop-up—a batted ball hit high in the air and almost directly above the infield or shallow outfield.

Presentation—a holding or stopped position the pitcher takes just before beginning his or her windup.

Pull hitter—a batter who consistently hits to one side of the field; that is, a right-handed hitter who always hits to left field or a left-handed hitter who consistently hits to right field.

Putout—a play other than a strike-out in which the hitter or baserunner is called out.

Quick hands—the ability to field and throw the ball quickly and efficiently.

Relay man—a fielder, usually an infielder, who takes a throw from an outfielder and throws it on to another infielder.

Relay throw—the throw made to the relay man or the throw made by the relay man.

Rise ball—a pitched ball that deviates from a straight line, moving upward.

Rundown—a defensive play in which one or more players attempt to tag a baserunner who is trapped between bases.

Sacrifice bunt—an offensive play in which the batter taps (bunts) a pitched ball fairly to advance a runner even though he will most likely be put out himself.

Screwball—a pitched ball that moves in toward a batter, also called an in-shoot.

Second sacker—the second baseman.

Shin guards—protective devices, which are strapped to the front of the catcher's lower legs and knees.

Shortstop—the player who plays between second and third base.

Sign—a visible movement of the hand, arm, or leg (a code) by a coach. This code tells the hitter or the runner or both what to do on a certain pitch.

Signal—a visible code from catcher to pitcher that tells the pitcher what pitch to throw. It is usually given with the fingers of the throwing hand.

Single—a base hit by a batter that advances him or her to first base.

Slingshot—a style of delivery used by pitchers in fast pitch.

Spikes—metal, rubber, or plastic cleats attached to a player's shoes to give better footing.

Squares around—settles into position. The position a batter takes in preparing to place a sacrifice bunt.

Square stance—a position taken by a batter as he prepares to hit; both feet are the same distance from the plate.

Squeeze play—an offensive move used when a runner is on third base. As the ball is pitched, the runner immediately runs for home plate and the hitter bunts the ball (fast pitch only).

Steal—an offensive move in which the runner leaves with the pitch and attempts to advance without being thrown out by the catcher (fast pitch only).

Steals signal—a strategy move whereby one team learns the other team's code. For example, a baserunner could detect the catcher's signal to the pitcher.

Steps in bucket—an incorrect stride by a batter in which he steps away from the pitch rather than striding straight ahead.

Straight-in slide—a move by a runner to avoid a tag by sliding straight into the base.

Stretching a hit—an attempt by a hitter to try for an additional base.

Strike zone (fast pitch)—the zone in which a pitched ball passes over any part of home plate between the batter's armpits and the top of his knees when the batter assumes his natural batting stance.

Strike zone (slow pitch)—the zone in which a

pitched ball passes over any part of home plate between the batter's highest shoulder and his knees when the batter assumes his natural batting stance.

Stuff—the movement or break of the pitched ball; that is, curve, drop, rise ball, in-shoot, change-up, etc.

Tag (out)—a putout completed by a fielder touching the runner with the ball.

Third sacker—the third baseman.

Topped ball—a batted ball hit at the top by the batter, which causes it to bounce on the ground.

Triple—a three-base hit.

Walk—the awarding of first base by the umpire after he has called four "balls."

Warm-up—the time used in exercise by a pitcher or other players in preparing to play.

Windmill—a type of pitching style in fast pitch.

Wind sprint—fast running for a short distance by a player in warming up.

Windup—a movement of the pitcher's arms and body in preparation for delivering the ball to a batter.

ASA 3 Teams

3

Winners' Bracket

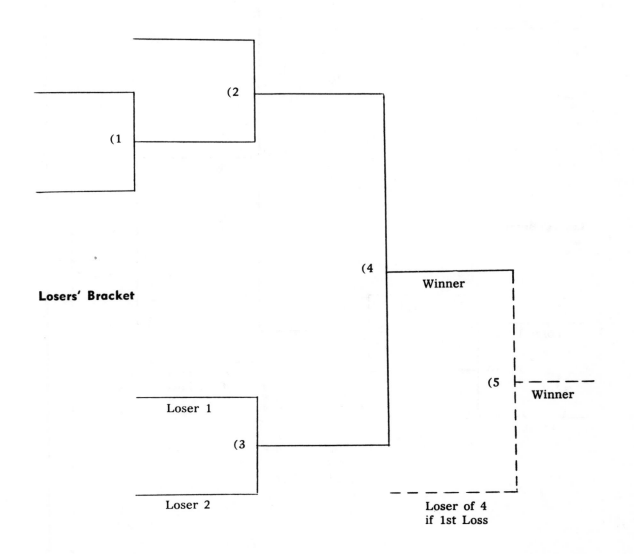

(1

(2

(4

Winner

Losers' Bracket

Loser 1

(3

Loser 2

(5

Winner

Loser of 4
if 1st Loss

Winners' Bracket

Losers' Bracket

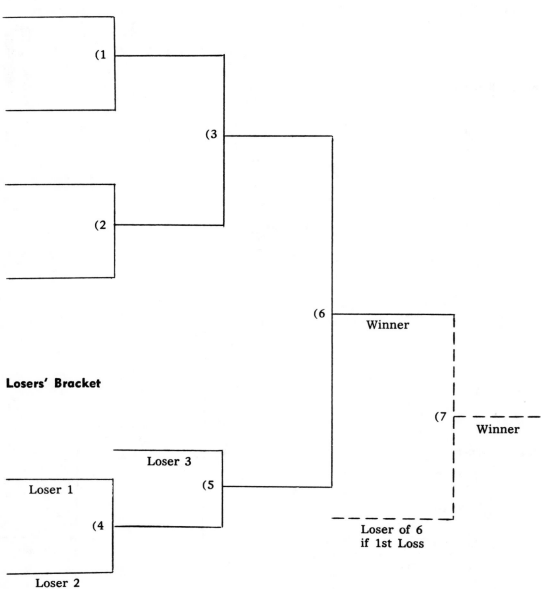

ASA 5 Teams

5

Winners' Bracket

Losers' Bracket

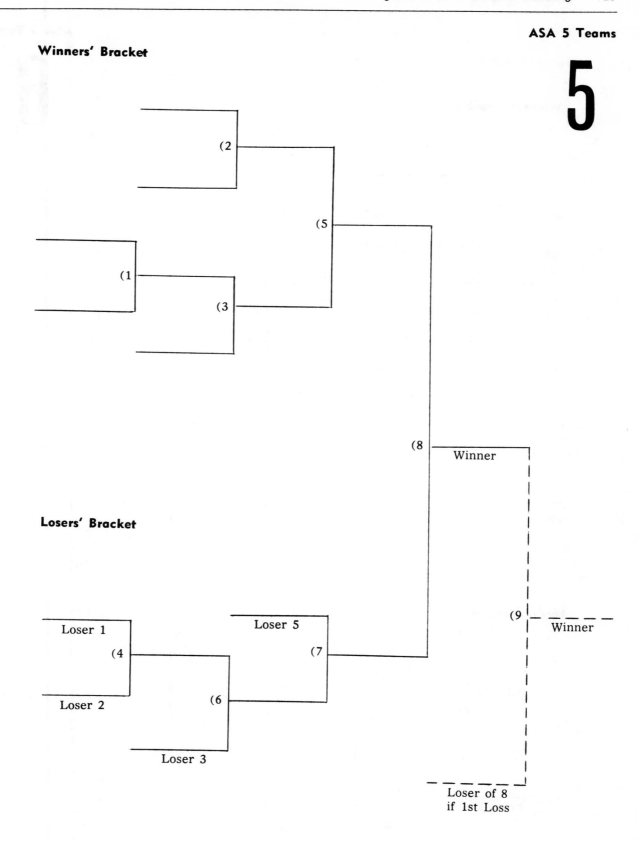

Winners' Bracket

Losers' Bracket

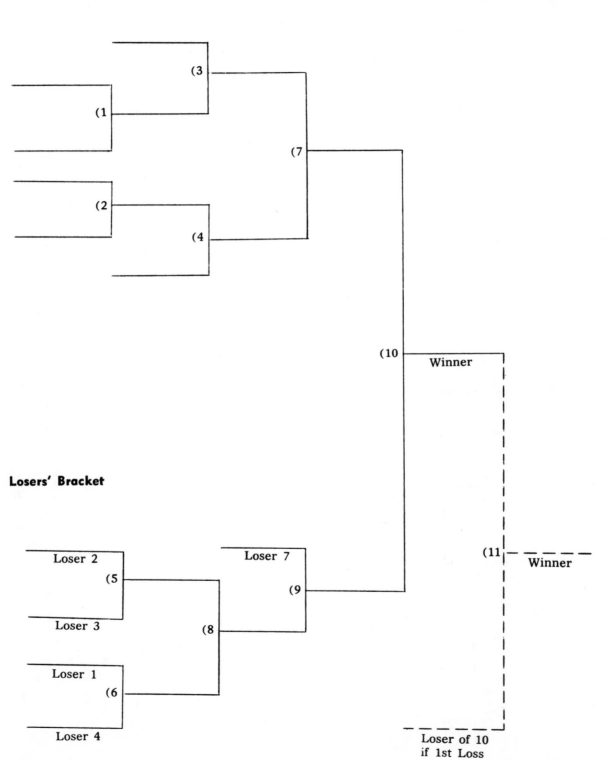

Winners' Bracket

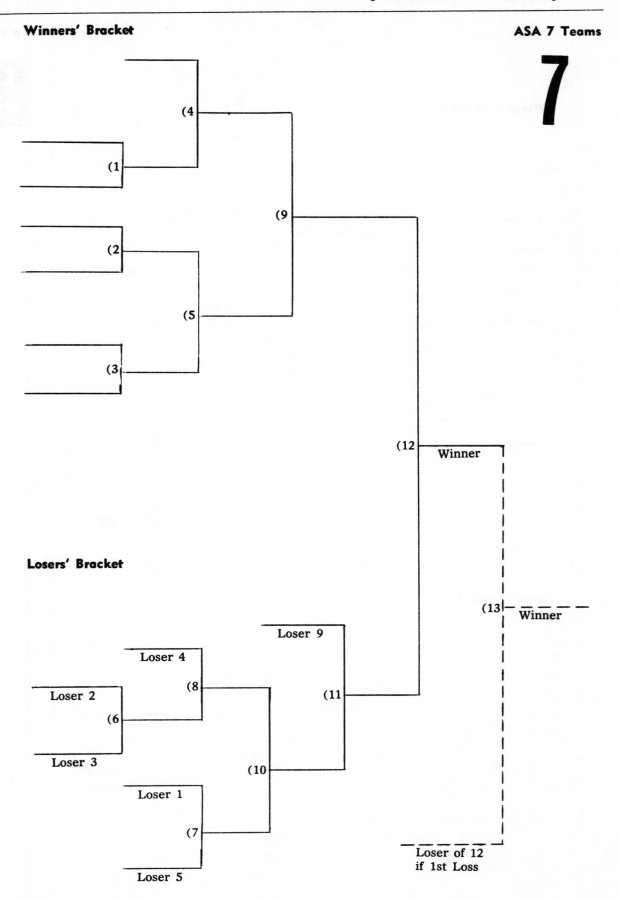

(4

(1

(2

(5

(3

(9

(12   Winner

(13   Winner

Losers' Bracket

Loser 9

Loser 4

(8

Loser 2

(6

Loser 3

(11

(10

Loser 1

(7

Loser 5

Loser of 12
if 1st Loss

Winners' Bracket

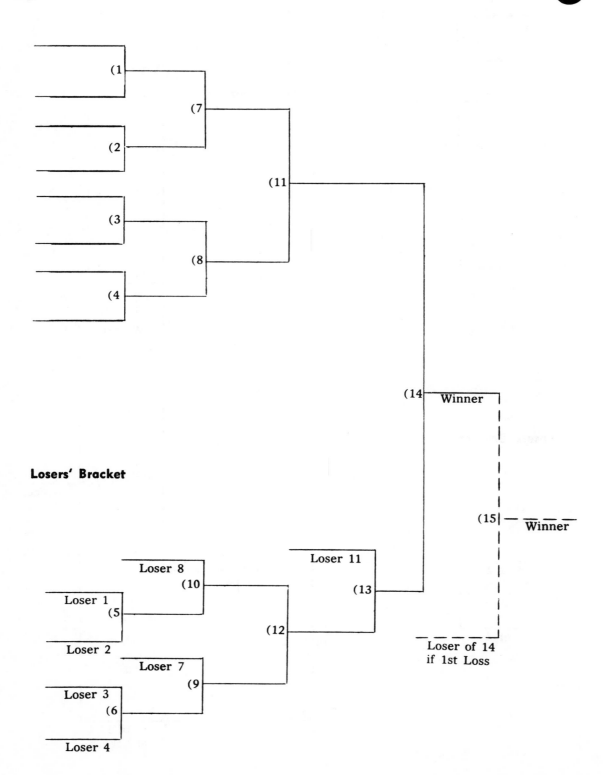

Losers' Bracket

Winners' Bracket

Losers' Bracket

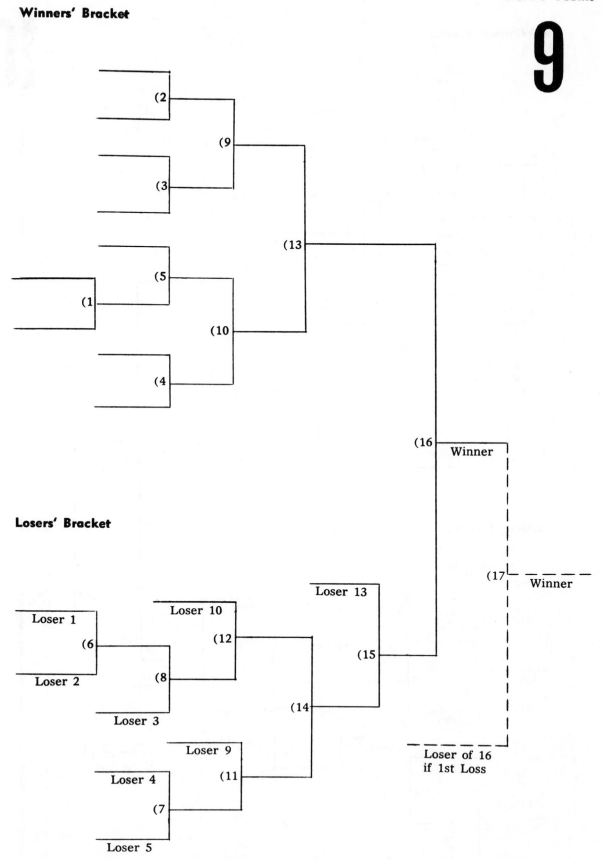

Winners' Bracket

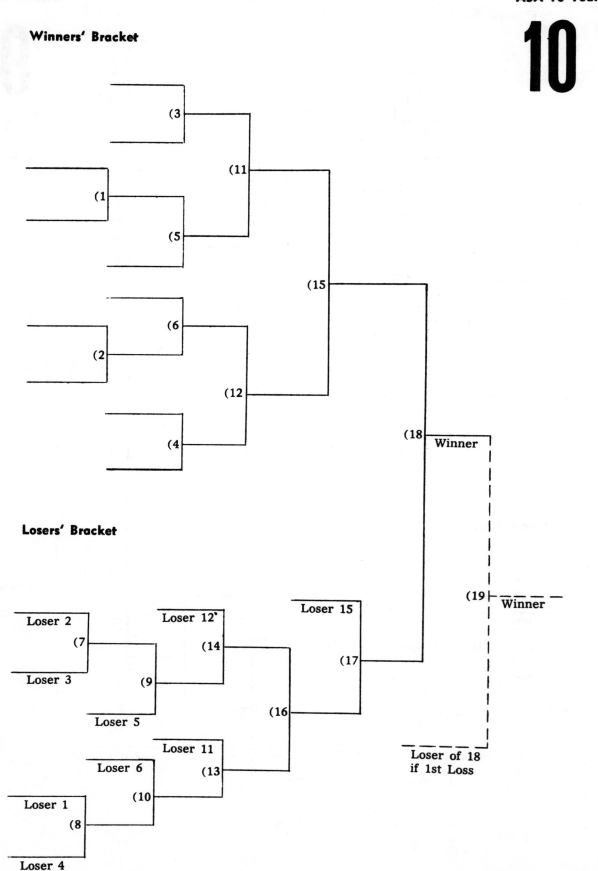

Losers' Bracket

Winners' Bracket

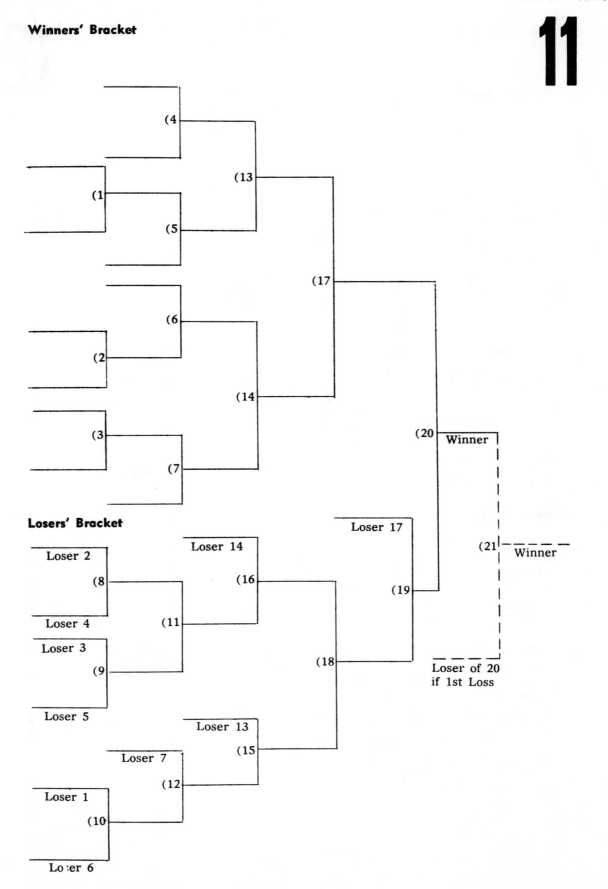

Losers' Bracket

Winners' Bracket

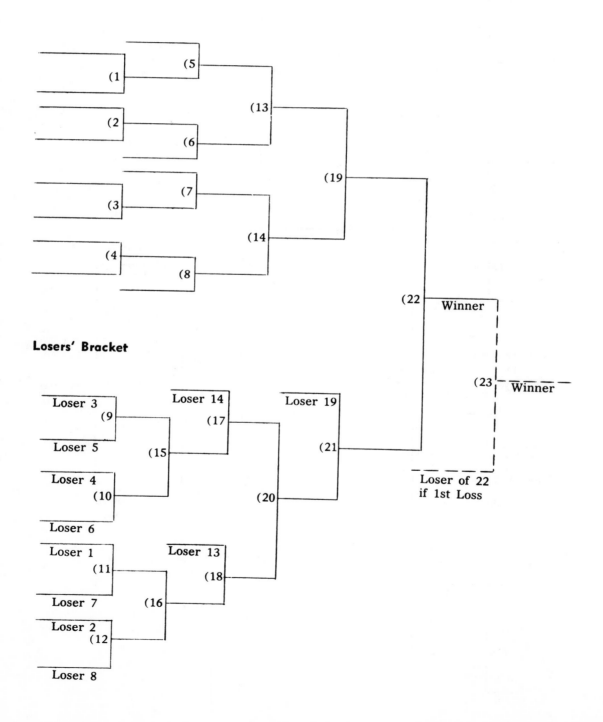

Losers' Bracket

ASA 13 Teams

13

Winners' Bracket

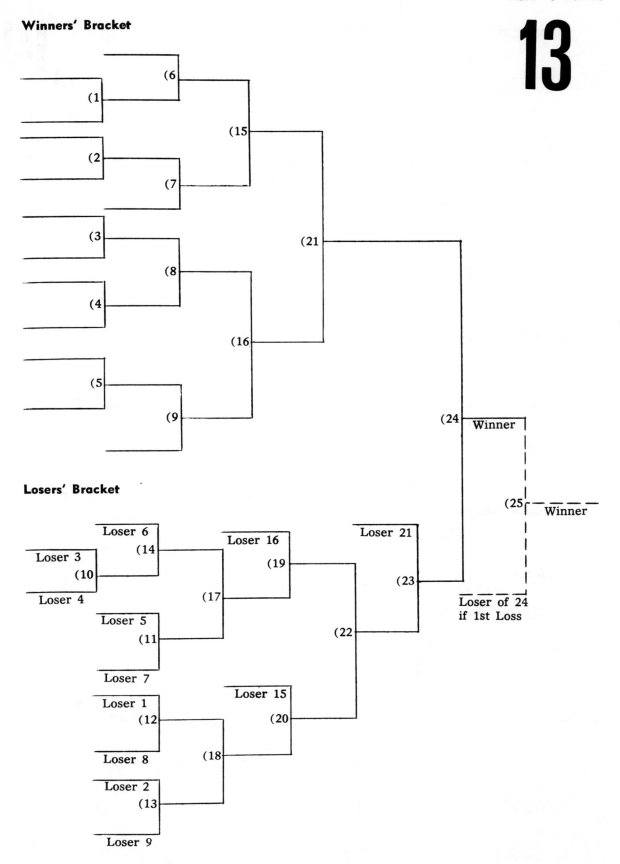

Losers' Bracket

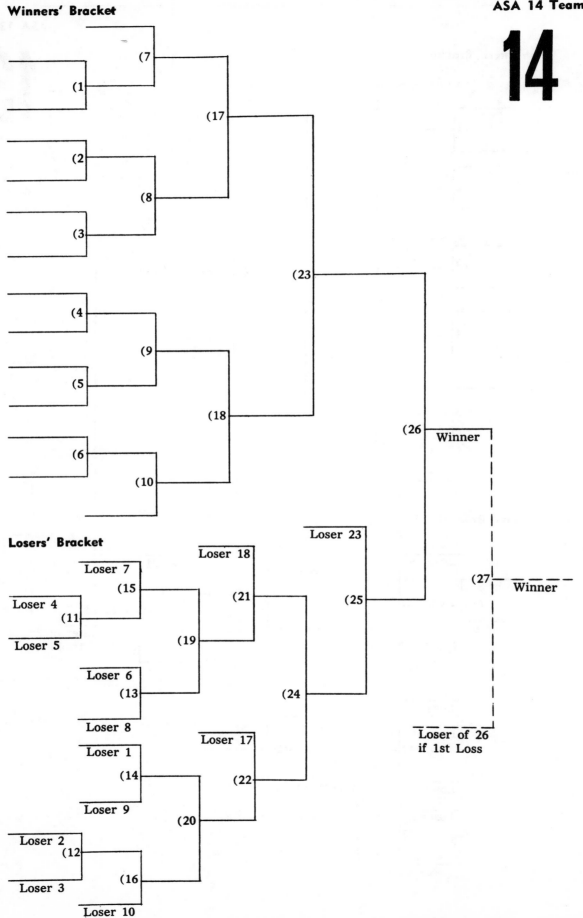

Winners' Bracket

ASA 14 Teams

14

(7
(1

(2
(8
(3

(17

(4
(9
(5

(18

(6
(10

(23

(26   Winner

Losers' Bracket

Loser 23

Loser 7
(15
Loser 4
(11
Loser 5

Loser 18

(21

(19

Loser 6
(13
Loser 8

(25

(24

(27   Winner

Loser 1
(14
Loser 9

Loser 17

(22

(20

Loser 2
(12
Loser 3

(16

Loser 10

Loser of 26
if 1st Loss

Winners' Bracket

(8

(1

(19

(2

(9

(3

(25

(4

(10

(5

(20

(6

(11

(7

(28   Winner

Losers' Bracket

Loser 20

Loser 25

Loser 8
(16

Loser 4
(12

Loser 5

(23

(21

(27

Loser 6
(13

Loser 7

(17

Loser 9

(26

(29   Winner

Loser 19

Loser 1
(15

Loser 10

(24

(22

Loser 2
(14

Loser 3

(18

Loser 11

Loser of 28
if 1st Loss

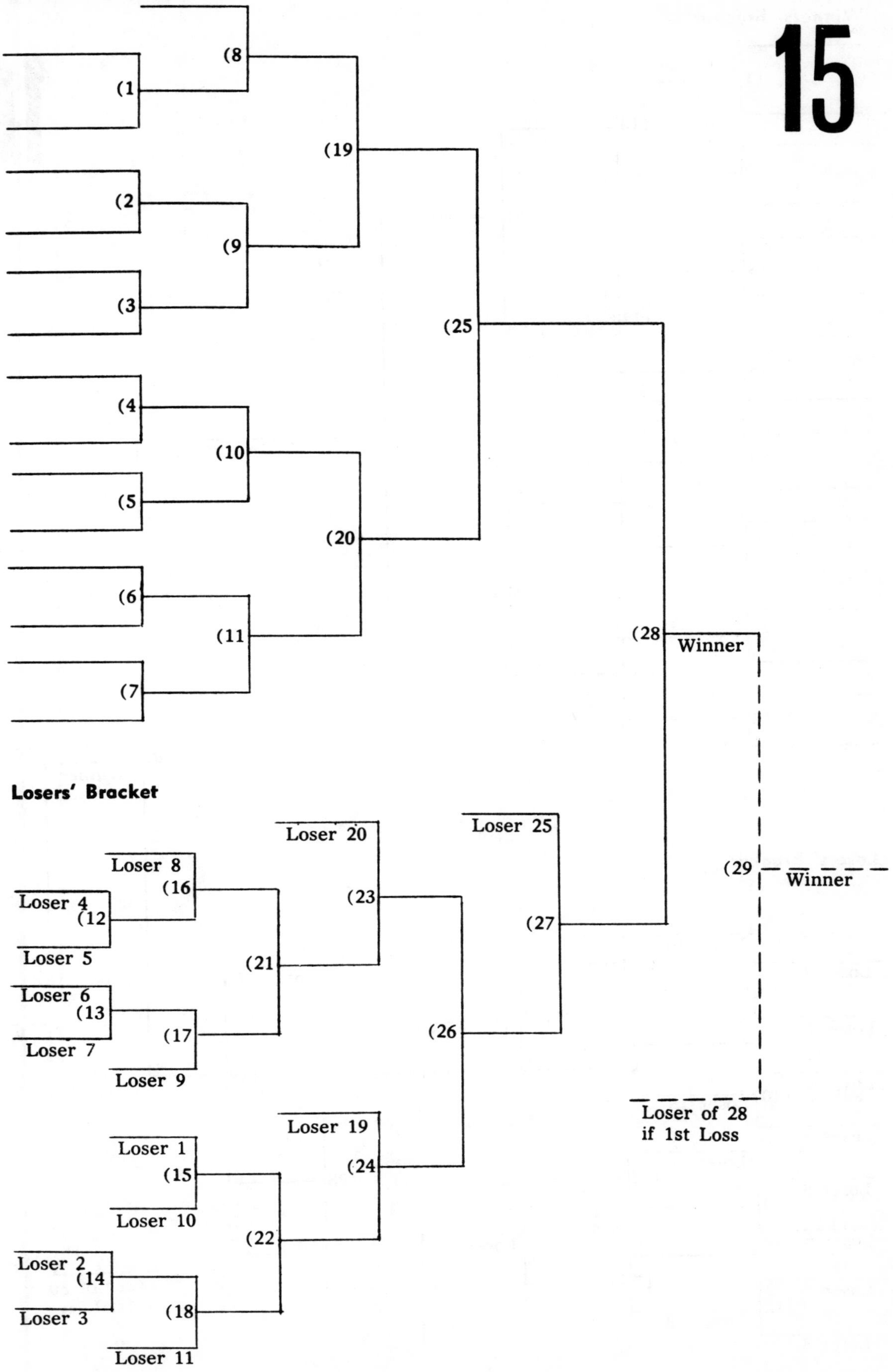

ASA 16 Teams

16

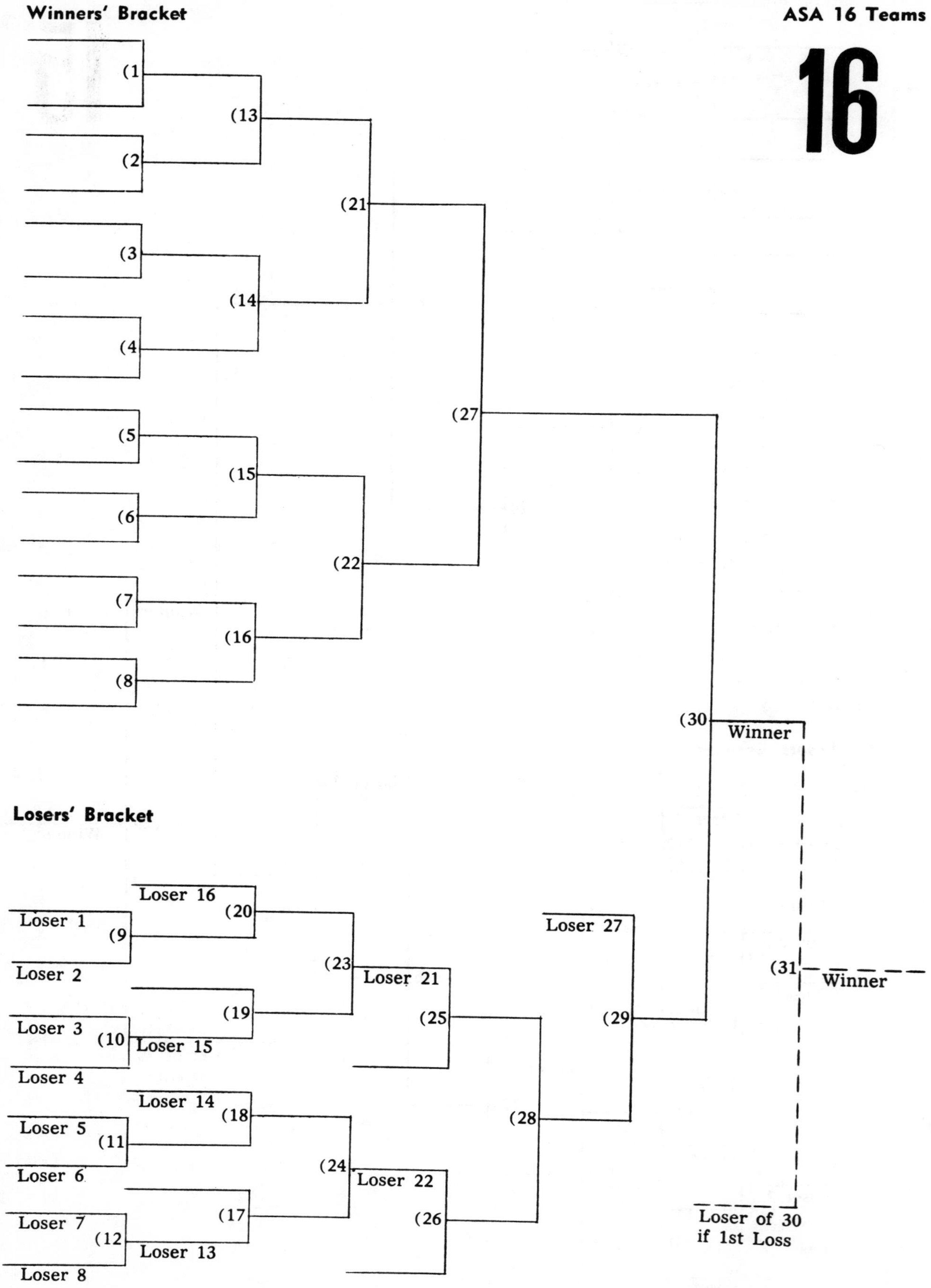
Winners' Bracket
(1
(2
(3
(4
(5
(6
(7
(8
(13
(14
(15
(16
(21
(22
(27
(30
Winner
Losers' Bracket
Loser 16
(20
Loser 1
(9
Loser 2
(19
Loser 3
(10
Loser 15
Loser 4
Loser 14
(18
Loser 5
(11
Loser 6
(17
Loser 7
(12
Loser 13
Loser 8
(23
Loser 21
(25
(24
Loser 22
(26
(28
Loser 27
(29
(31
Winner
Loser of 30
if 1st Loss

Winners' Bracket

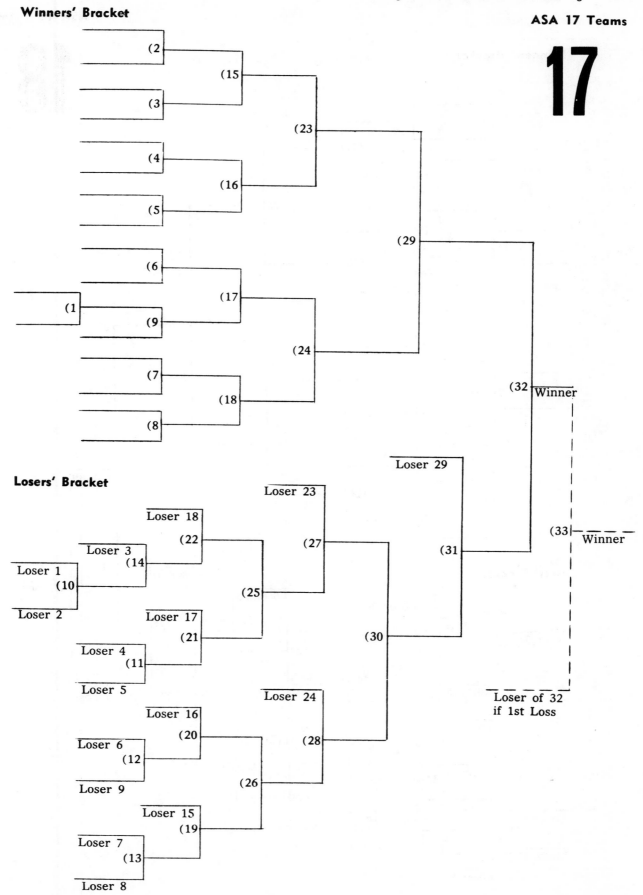

Losers' Bracket

Winners' Bracket

Losers' Bracket

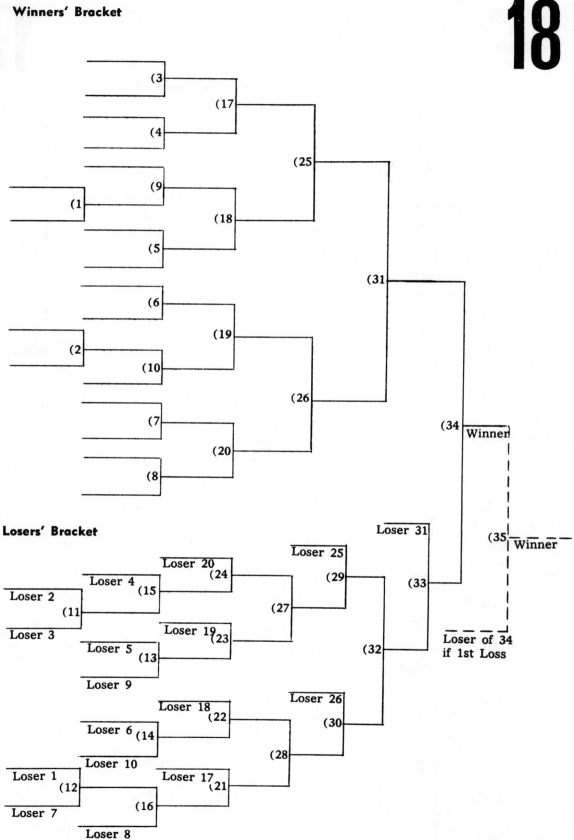

Winners' Bracket

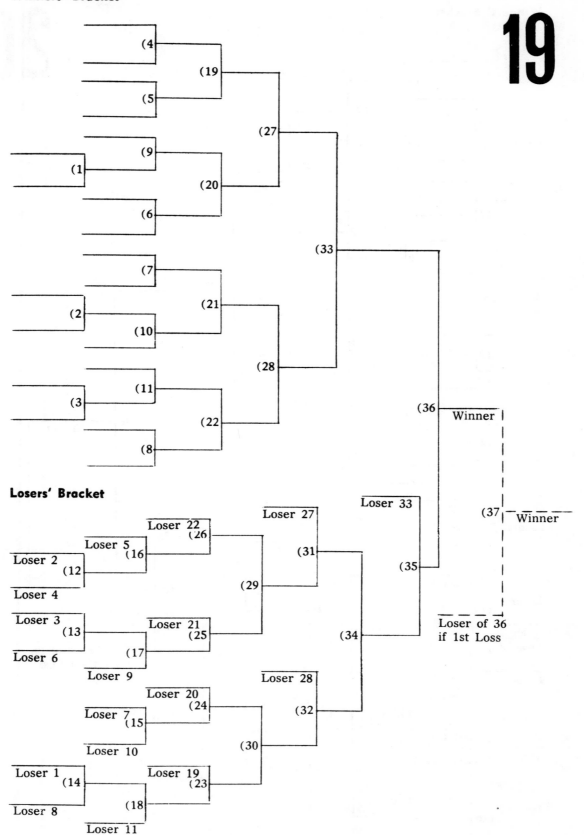

19

Losers' Bracket

Winners' Bracket

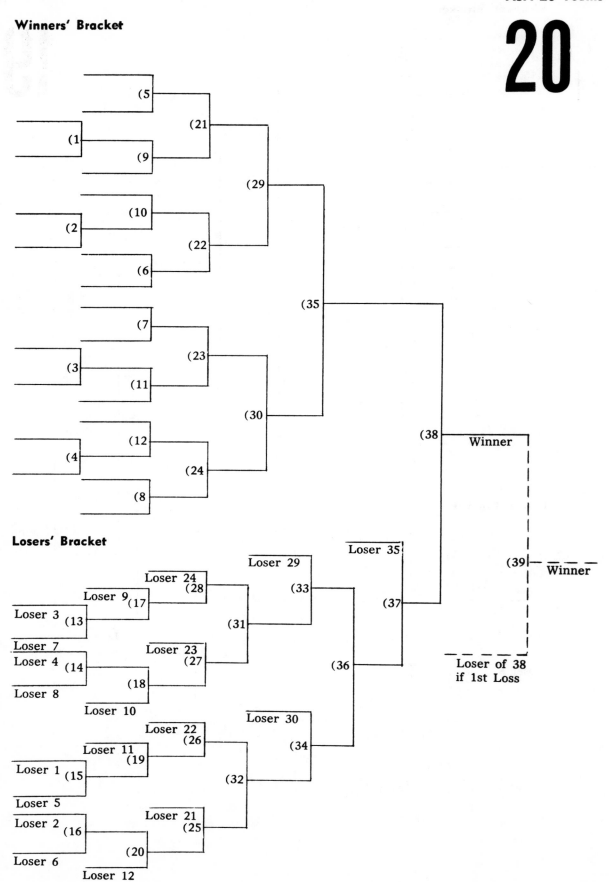

Losers' Bracket

Index